TREADING WATER

Holding Weights

TACKLING AND EMBRACING THE CHAOS OF MOTHERHOOD

MELISSA KUSHNARYOV

Published by Melissa Kushnaryov

Published by Melissa Kushnaryov
Carlsbad, CA
www.melissakushnaryov.com

Printed in the United States of America

Creative direction by Dan Saal, Wonderfull Design
Cover and page design by Erika Brask
Page layout by Dan Saal, Wonderfull Design
Photos by Melissa and Anton Kushnaryov

ISBN: 978-1-7354695-0-8

For Anton.

Thank you for joining me on this wild ride
and for lifting me up when I need it most.

I love you.

CONTENTS

Introduction

Hold on, moms. Are you sure you have time to read a book? You sure? Can you sneak in a few paragraphs during naps? Perhaps while the kiddos are eating? Maybe even after you put them all to sleep and your haggard self tosses the dishes in the dishwasher, kicks some Cheerios under the table and collapses on the couch. Yeah, you're right. There are probably a few moments here and there. So, maybe you'll get through this book in approximately 11 months. But it'll be worth it.

Time is way too precious for moms, I know that. So here's my commitment to you with this book you're about to read: I promise to make it worth it for you. Yes! If you read this, it'll be a good use of that "spare time" while the kids play with Duplo blocks and smear soggy goldfish into the carpet.

Here's what I'm going to do for you with these pages: I'm going to be really honest with you about motherhood as I've experienced it. I won't sugarcoat anything, which will hopefully be refreshing. There's just too much crap out there about being supermoms and balancing it all and having it all together. We're expected to cheerfully build human beings inside our bodies, extrude them from our loins with poise, raise them to be respectable humans and calmly tell them they hurt our feelings when they bite us on the saggy skin where our triceps are supposed to be. Motherhood is real and raw and there's nothing wrong with talking honestly about it. So, let's do just that.

But on top of this, I'm also going to give you some little nuggets of wisdom to help you navigate motherhood. Use the advice you find in this book that works for you, and ignore the advice that doesn't. The good news is that millions of women have forged this frontier before, and there are some great pieces of insight that we can pass down. We are all doing our best at this mom thing, and our best is just fine. There's no perfection here. It's not even a thing in motherhood.

As soon as we embrace the fact that perfection isn't even an option, we can all breathe a little deeper.

Oh, and thank you. I know there are a lot of amazing books out there that are written by fabulous women talking about this same thing: the madness of motherhood. I don't take it lightly that you decided to open up this one. Thanks for trusting your precious "free time" (which isn't even a thing when you're a mom) with me and the pages that follow!

xx Melissa

P.S. You'll notice that there are many excerpts throughout this book that are taken from social media, blog posts and stories I've written. These are not in chronological order. They're pulled from pieces I've written over the past few years. Enjoy!

CHAPTER ONE

Children are Chaos: And there's not much you can do about it.

There's not really a better way to start this book, or this exact chapter really, than what I just experienced. I poured myself a glass of wine and sat down to start typing away. The kids are asleep, my husband is at his drawing class (which is actually hilariously called "The 7 Key Folds of Drapery", but more about that later) and I had time and space and peace. I opened my computer and started typing. Then my youngest started screaming.

See, I put the kids all to sleep in one big bed tonight, thinking I'd sort them out into their own beds when I went to bed, so the little one screaming was definitely a CODE RED problem. I ran down the hall. I thought to myself 'kick off those slippers, you'll be more agile!' I kicked off those slippers. I hurried into the room, forgot my phone so I couldn't see a single thing, jumped onto my oldest son's ankle, woke him up, rolled over my middle child's face, woke her up, and grabbed my screaming baby by the elbow, which he hated.

I wasn't agile. Perhaps I was 15 years ago. I can't remember.

I threw them all into their beds, sung songs, got water, snuggled, told stories, rubbed backs, flipped pillows, flattened covers, flipped pillows, shushed, flipped goddamn pillows, and finally got them all back to sleep. I had just done all of this about 20 minutes ago. And this is motherhood.

It's just chaos. All of it is chaos. But we're all going through it. Everyone with little kids is chewing on a bit of chaos right now, and they'll chew on it tonight at midnight, then again at 2am, 4am, maybe 6am and all through tomorrow. There's nothing we can do about it. But we signed up for this. We didn't realize what we were signing up for, but we did, in fact, sign up for this.

. . . .

INSTAGRAM POST AUGUST 14, 2018

You know what's happening at bedtime at our house these days!? More drama than anyone should have to face at the end of a day. My kids are adamant about going to bed with ice packs. That's right. It gets weird here once the sun goes down.

We had a heat wave. HAD. The heat wave is very much over, and it has returned to normal temperatures again. However, my children are so caught up in the drama of the heat wave. They're so consumed by the elaborate and ridiculous bedtime routine we used during the heat wave, that they cannot even begin to realize that it's not hot anymore. Their insanity has taken over and reason has been thrown out the window.

 TREADING WATER, HOLDING WEIGHTS

So I have to prepare for battle every night before I walk into their room. I grab six wet wash cloths (yes, six), two ice packs and two cups of water. My kids sprawl out on their tummies and I meticulously line their backs with the wet wash cloths. Then I carefully lay the packs on the wash cloths. The slightest move and my services are required again. The placement is very important. Very precise.

Then I sit and wait for Miela to scream that she's hungry, because she always does, even when I feed her right before bed. And by now I've figured out that she means thirsty. Luckily I always come prepared. This isn't my first rodeo.

Then, of course, Toren needs water too because one can't have something without the other needing it, obviously. Hence the cups of water. They can't share. Then I'm back to carefully repositioning the wet wash cloths and ice packs, because of course all of my meticulous work was ruined when the thirst alarm went off.

Then come the music requests. Toren will only fall asleep to one particular song. So I turn on Spotify and play it over and over again. He sings every word and drifts off. It's adorable. So one is out. Not bad. Keep going mama!

But Miela is never ready to give in so easily. She needs to hear nature sounds, specifically birds chirping. Luckily, Spotify has that too. But she also wants to hear squirrels. Spotify doesn't have that. No one does. So she falls asleep every night trying desperately to hear the squirrels among the birds. They aren't there, but she doesn't need to know. That'll be our little secret for now. (Listen for them Miela. Do you hear them? There! That was one! You missed it? Shhh...keep listening.)

And that's what I'm doing between 8:15 and 9 at night. So this evening while you're watching Netflix and drinking some Pinot, think of me and the squirrels and the little girl falling asleep with her finger in my belly button because, well, that's a non-negotiable with this 2 year old.

. . . .

Even when things get crazy, there are the cute moments buried in there. It can be adorable and sweet, but it also makes me want to smack my head against the walls on occasion, just to make sure this is all real.

You know, I often wonder when my children will develop a sense of self preservation. This has to be a thing that human beings develop sooner or later. I developed it, and I bet you did too. But my children haven't gotten there yet.

It's like they're attracted to horrible ideas. My son stacked up two laundry baskets, then balanced a chair on top of them, and then sat on that chair. I walked into the room and couldn't speak out of fear that he'd get startled and tumble down. It's almost impossible to live your life when the person you hold dearest to your heart is attempting death-defying feats on the hour.

But that's how it is. If your child isn't a daredevil, then you get another dose of chaos. My daughter screams and howls at every chance. She's a normal, happy, energetic child who seems quite sociable and enjoyable. The moment she sees a little opening, the glimmer of a chance to scream and throw a fit, she tosses in all of her chips, exploding in a dramatic display of complete devastation. She lives for these moments.

It's almost impossible to live your life when the person you hold dearest to your heart is attempting death-defying feats on the hour.

 TREADING WATER, HOLDING WEIGHTS

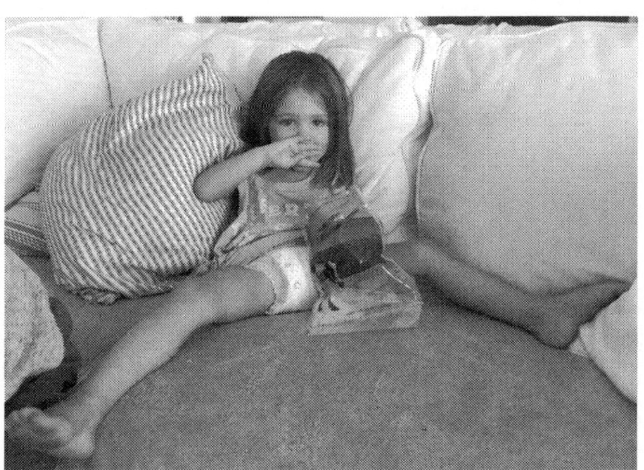

Miela at two years old. Today we caught her eating a bag of shredded cheese on the couch. She sat there with the bag between her legs, wearing her brother's enormous t-shirt and no pants. I get it girl, eating lots of cheese on the couch without pants on sounds luxurious sometimes, but that was for tacos tonight. Somehow you nearly downed the whole bag. I can't make any promises about what this will do to your digestion.

She's been walking around the house for two days screaming that her foot is bleeding and she needs to go to the hospital. It's not bleeding. I can't find a single scratch or bruise on it. This morning she adamantly accused the baby of holding a knife and broke out into hysterics. I checked out her story. As suspected, it doesn't check out.

She refuses to wear shoes at all times. She likes to try to scare us by telling us there are 'pelicans and yarks' behind us, and that they're going to 'get us'. She means skeletons and sharks. If she comes up behind me one more time while I'm doing the dishes and screams 'The pelicans and yarks are coming for you!' I can't promise that I'll respond sensibly. This mama can keep her cool for only so long, and the pelicans and yarks are pushing me near the edge.

She likes to hand me things and tell me not to put them down, ever. Then she stands about five feet from me and watches to make sure I don't put them down... ever. She is very patient at this game, and there is no waiting her out.

She has started fighting back when her older brother picks on her. She does some sort of slow-mo kung fu moves with her arms while slowly walking towards him. Then, when she gets within striking distance, she kicks him in the legs.

She refuses to fall asleep at night unless her finger is IN MY BELLY BUTTON.

Two year olds are so strange, so funny and absolutely payback for all of the craziness I put my mom through when I was little.

. . . .

I'm pretty sure I was the exact same way. I know I was.

These little brains are absorbing so much every day. They are processing and evaluating and understanding. They experience many firsts and are trying to fit the puzzle pieces together. With all of this learning comes a deep desire for independence and identity. They may still want to be under our wing, but they're putting feelers out and trying to figure out how they fit into this world.

It's scary for them. The world is so big, endlessly huge to them. These children of ours are trying to make sense of it all with brains that haven't developed yet. It's hard. But it's ok because they have us. Right?

Yes, mama, they have us.

We have their backs. We love them endlessly and eternally. The very thought of anything happening to them grips our bellies and takes the breath from our bodies. We couldn't even imagine.

So why do they poop in our shoes and shove macaroni up their noses? Why do they hide grapes in the couch cushions and intentionally drop their socks out of the stroller when we aren't looking?

There are some questions we will never know the answers to, and that's ok. We can't control it all. But we can control how we respond, right?

We can control how much we let it all get to us. We can control our expectations and the pressures we let ourselves feel. The world is constantly setting us up to fail and to feel inadequate. I'm not a pessimist. I'm

   TREADING WATER, HOLDING WEIGHTS

not. But I do know that society holds the unrealistic up on a pedestal, and that makes being a mother very hard.

I remember before I had my first child, I bought into this unrealistic version of motherhood. I had visions of myself as a mother. I knew I would never yell. I would instead calmly guide. I knew I would never show anger. I would instead be a deep breathing beacon of yoga light that spread my magical mom aura over all of my children. I would keep the peace and tranquility wafting through the house, no matter what. My child would not take over my life or rob me of my independence. These stories I heard of mothers letting themselves go and falling apart, that wouldn't be me. I would still run marathons and do yoga daily and eat only healthy meals made from scratch and keep my career going strong. I would be the perfect mom who is there for absolutely everything. I would see all of my friends. We would take the longest, most peaceful walks through the park while I listened to podcasts and started a company and wrote a book and kept my marriage hot and steamy through it all. I never would have admitted any of this to you, or even to myself. But looking back, I know that's what I expected.

After 46 hours of intense labor that left me unable to walk down the street for two weeks, I began to think that maybe things were going to be a bit different than I had expected.

After hanging up my marathon shoes because I couldn't run without peeing, I started to wonder if I was doing something wrong.

After calling my mom every morning on the brink of tears, asking her if I was ever going to sleep again, I thought that maybe I was a horrible mother.

She assured me, as a mother of six does, that I would make it. My father yelled in the background from his recliner that "this too shall pass" and "you'll have a better day tomorrow" and "life is hard and then you die". They told me to ease up on my expectations, to try to do just one thing

...society holds the unrealistic up on a pedestal, and that makes being a mother very hard.

every day. They weren't saying to try to get out of the house and accomplish one thing every day. They were saying to literally just have one thing planned for every day. Like, Monday could be the day I was going to do a load of laundry, just one. That's where they told me to start.

And it felt good. It felt good to have an expert mother tell me to dial it all back and do less. I was relieved to hear that simplifying was the way to go. My mom told me I was insane to insist on a two mile walk every day when I couldn't even sleep a solid hour at a time during the night. I was finally able to take a deep breath when she told me that I was doing just fine and wasn't a horrible mother.

See, there's not one way to do it. There's not one way to be a good mother or one way to raise fabulous children. There a billion ways and we're all just doing our best to find our own way here.

You have to find your own version of motherhood. And I do too. And so does that mom over there. And probably all of them include cleaning poop out of the carpet and wiping snotty noses with our own shirtsleeves. You can't get away from stuff like that.

If we are searching for perfection in motherhood, then we are searching for the impossible. That sounds exhausting. I don't need anything else sucking my energy. My kids have that job nailed down. But this search for perfection and excellence through all of the chaos—this search has me quite exhausted and, quite frankly, annoyed.

Let's be honest about a few things here. Motherhood consumes you and then you crawl out of the fog and you are forever changed, and it's great. It's also maddening.

My third is fabulous in every way, and also sweet and adorable. But he keeps me on my toes, all ten of them, all the time. The exhaustion is real over here.

I've begun to notice more grey hairs popping up and more wrinkles setting in. Some days I get really close to the mirror just to see if I'm still there. The good news is that I am. I'm still there. We all are.

The other day someone said to me, 'You look great for 36.' And hey, that sounds like a compliment. But the first thing that comes to mind is 'Wait, what is 36 supposed to look like?' And that's quickly followed with, 'Wait again. Did you just say 36?' I was just 32 and only 27 before that. I know I'm going to wake up tomorrow and be 58.

My third likes to run into streets and sprint towards the ocean. He would throw himself at that water if I'd let him. He likes to climb on tables and jump around on rocking chairs.

He does not try to eat pennies or get tangled in the cords of the shades on our windows. No, that stuff is too beginner level for him. Instead he climbs up on our chairs and lies on his back, dangling his head over the edge a little too far. He looks at me upside down with a very sly smile, and I know for sure that he's thinking 'There's a very good chance this won't end well mom. What are you going to do about it?' I could rush over and pull him down, but then I'd be living every moment of my life pulling him from potential disaster. Or I could stand back, close enough to maybe catch him if things go south, but far enough away so that he thinks I'm not affected by his terrifying act.

I usually choose to stand back. It's scary, but I'm sure there are important life lessons in that. Also, I have dishes to do and can't run around catching falling children all day.

. . . .

I once saw a mother's Instagram photo of her child's perfect bedroom. It was clean and white and super tidy. The photo showed a table and some macrame thing hanging from the pristine wall. For a moment, I thought, 'Wow, my kids' rooms don't look like that.' But should they!? Surely all of life's challenges would be fixed if my son's bedroom had a macrame on the wall. I ran out and bought yarn.

We are so quick to curate our lives for the camera, for social media. . . . What is it saying about the lives we really live? It's saying these lives aren't enough.

   Treading Water, Holding Weights

Then I got a vision of everything just beyond the camera shot, every-thing just beyond the lens. And it was glorious chaos. Toys were every-where. Clothes were tossed around. Half-eaten apples were on the floor by the door. It was exactly like my kids' rooms. Now, maybe that wasn't reality. Perhaps her macrame room was clean and tidy and spotless. But perhaps it wasn't! Perhaps the disaster was lurking just beyond the camera lens. And perhaps her kids were lurking there too, watching their mom create a false reality, pretending it was real life. And what message does that tell them?

And what does that mean for this perfect, macrame mama? We are so quick to curate our lives for the camera, for social media. But what is that saying about the real chaos? What is it saying about the lives we really live? It's saying these lives aren't enough. It's saying we aren't doing it right.

But we are.

Mama, we are.

. . . .

INSTAGRAM POST SEPTEMBER 27, 2018

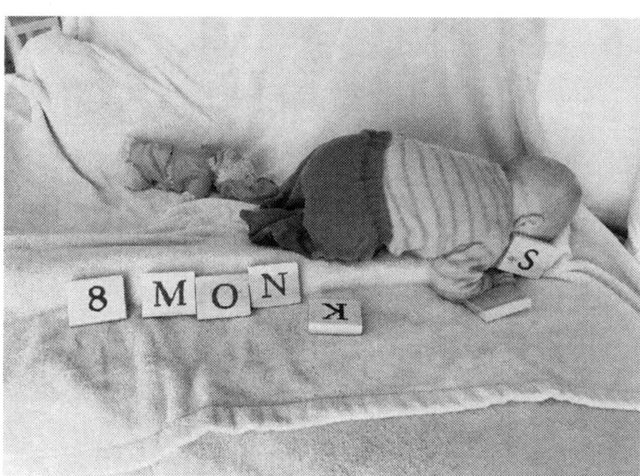

I'm looking for someone who can do just a bit of Photoshop work for me. Nothing crazy. Just some small edits on Karoh's eight month photo.

First of all, can you make him sit up? Ideally get his face looking at the camera with a huge smile. He doesn't have teeth yet, but you could add a few in there if it makes the smile look more legit. Have him holding that bear in his arms. Make it look like he really likes the bear, but not too much emotion so it looks like he's overly attached to it. Something like 'Oh, I'm a super happy boy and this bear is so cute and my mom doesn't ever let me eat food off the floor or sit around in a wet diaper.'

Obviously get the blocks right. It should say '8 MONTHS'. Maybe find a new font for the letters? Something a little more hipster, but in a 'I just threw this together' sort of way.

Actually, let's get rid of the blocks and the couch. Put him in front of a really cool mural at, like, a great coffee shop or something.

Put a chalkboard next to him that says something like 'I'm 8 months old!' And then list out all of the milestones he's passing by. But let's put in developmental milestones for, like, a two year old, so it looks like I'm really crushing it. I mean he's really crushing it. His head is at about a 65%. Can you bring it down to 50%? Actually, that's too perfect. Make it 52%, so it's kind of like 'Oh yeah, he has such a big head!' But it's only 2% so that's not really anything and maybe just room for more brains.

Different clothes, of course. Maybe pants and a jacket, a little bow tie and a hat? Just something that goes with the setting...the coffee shop and mural, not the couch.

Show him making an 'accidental', but super casual peace sign with his hand. Just something that kind of looks like he gets it, but obviously he's a baby so he doesn't, so make it look accidental.

Let me know if anyone has a couple of minutes to knock this out. I'd really like to get this picture up on social media today, but don't want to do that without these quick edits first.

 TREADING WATER, HOLDING WEIGHTS

Oh yeah, and date it about eight days ago, because he turned eight months a while ago, so I'll post this as a Throw Back Thursday even though I just snapped it. Does Venmo work?

. . . .

The chaos isn't something to hide, it's something to embrace and move through. Instead of doing all that we can to hide the crazy, what if we let it shine? What if we released the shame in motherhood and instead made it a beautiful thing?

Let's remember that kids are wild little animals. Our children, however we try to guide them, will naturally veer towards disorder. That glass of milk on the table, the one we set down by them thinking 'Maybe they won't spill this one, especially if I put it closer to the middle of the table, just a tad to their right side so they can easily grab it. Maybe they won't spill this one.' We even say to them, 'Don't spill your milk, honey.' Of course they spill it.

They don't just knock it over a little bit, they accidentally hurl it across the table onto our plate with our sandwich and also somehow onto our phone sitting next to our plate with our soggy milk sandwich. This is how they naturally live: accidentally and enthusiastically moving towards chaos.

We do what we can to avoid these daily disasters, but they are inevitable. Even if we put a top on their cup of milk, they'll veer away from that mishap and instead tumble out of their chair for no reason, or get their fork stuck in their sweater or drag a chunk of hair though their yogurt. This is what happens. Eventually this becomes normal life.

So your child has yogurt in their hair and a fork stuck in their sweater and you're trying to eat your milk sandwich. It's in these moments that you have to realize that none of this is avoidable. None of it.

What if we released the shame in motherhood and instead made it a beautiful thing?

But everything IS going to be ok, and everyone IS going to make it, as long as you get that fork out of that sweater at some point. You can leave the yogurt for a couple of days.

I know it doesn't always seem that way though. The constant insanity and unpredictability that we're expected to live with, it's not easy to digest. And there's a bit of anxiety and disbelief that settles in every night after they fall asleep. At the end of some days, we just sit back in awe.

I believe there's an art to embracing this craziness that comes with motherhood. There's also an art to finding ways to avoid it. But it's never completely eluded. It shows up in one way or another. Even simple outings to the grocery store can end in complete madness.

. . . there's an art to embracing this craziness that comes with motherhood. There's also an art to finding ways to avoid it.

INSTAGRAM POST AUGUST 8, 2019

We went to the beach with buddies today. It felt good to get our feet and faces in the sand again. The beach always wears them out and usually sets us up for a legit nap time. But today no one napped after the beach. Brutal.

Around 3pm I tossed in the towel and we ran to the grocery store to get stuff for baking. Nothing is better than a bunch of exhausted kids at the grocery store and then heading back home to knock out some baking in the kitchen. It's the equivalent of letting a chicken peck at your infected toe for an hour. Horrendous, unimaginable and stupid. But that's how I like to roll.

We painfully cried, rolled, ran, yelled and had tantrums down the aisles of Von's grocery store. I had my list in hand and the determination of a mountain lion. Baking soda. Baking soda. Second to last thing on my list. Baking soda. Aisle 12: baking stuff. Where's the soda for baking?

I gave up and headed to aisle 1 for cheese. There I found a woman in a Von's shirt. She avoided my eyes, but I asked her anyways where the baking soda was. Her response was 'aisle 12'. 'Yes,' I said 'I looked and looked. But I just couldn't find it.'

Her response (as she pushed her restocking cart away from me with the speed of a mountain lion on the hunt), 'oh, I'll have to keep my eyes open for it.' She was gone before I could say another word.

You know what? I don't blame her. I was a scary sight. It would have been a messy trip to aisle 12. I'm not mad at you, Von's woman. I'm not mad at you.

But then I found a guy in a Von's shirt. He searched aisle 12 with me. We came up empty. 'Stay here', he said, 'I'll go ask customer service.' My little mountain lions were devouring each other and everything on the shelves by then, but I stayed put. I watched him walk up to 'Customer Service' and ask where the baking soda was.

And because the stars aligned and karma is most certainly a bitch at times, the customer service woman was indeed the woman in the Von's shirt who ran away from me. I saw her look over his shoulder at me, say 'aisle 12', and walk away.

I still don't blame her. Sometimes you have to avoid disasters in life in order to keep your own sanity. Keep your sanity, Von's woman. I lost mine years ago. You hold onto yours tightly.

. . . .

So how can you accept the tumultuous nature of childhood into your well managed adult life? How can you open the door to the unpredictable milk sandwiches of your future and not lose your shit every time they are tossed your way, which is daily?

I think we have to remember that "this too shall pass" and "you'll have a better day tomorrow" and "life is hard and then you die". The last one might be a bit harsh, so you can take it or leave it. The point is, there are things we can control and many things we cannot control in motherhood. Choosing, instead, to control how we react, now that's the real trick to sailing through the chaos and into whatever lies beyond it (which is most likely a different flavor of chaos, so brace yourself).

     TREADING WATER, HOLDING WEIGHTS

CHAPTER TWO

Everyone Struggles: Even the hip Instagram moms clean poop off their couches.

I once found myself sitting on the edge of a flower bed in a park nursing my baby, sunglasses on, crying because I was so tired and depleted. But the sunglasses, they came in handy and hid my disastrous state quite well. From a few feet away, I looked like a totally ok mom who had it together pretty well and was rocking this mom thing.

Then the sprinklers went on and I couldn't move because it was my first baby and I wasn't yet a breastfeeding ninja who could make a souffle, clean the floors and write Christmas cards all while nursing my totally calm and content baby.

No. This was my first. I was a nervous breastfeeding disaster. Milk went everywhere and I was terrified of my nipples popping out. (Oh the horror!) I absolutely could not move a muscle while I was nursing.

So when the sprinklers went on, I just sat there soaking wet and crying. I tried to keep up the appearance that everything was ok and that this whole scene was totally fine. No, no, I don't need help. Oh no, this is totally ok. Yeah, thanks, we're good. What's that? I'm soaking wet? Yeah, I know. It's ok.

We do this weird thing way too often. We force ourselves to hold our heads up high, slap smiles on our faces and pretend everything is 100% completely amazing all of the time. But it's hard. This is hard, and there's no shame in admitting that. In fact, I found that once I started opening up about the reality of my struggles in motherhood, the more connection I found with other mothers and the more at peace I was with my own self.

. . . .

INSTAGRAM POST JULY 17, 2018

I don't really have this motherhood thing down. Today I chatted with another mama about the disasters of motherhood and how some moms display an image of perfection on social media. I once had a close friend tell me that motherhood seemed to come so easily to me.

Here's the thing: I love being a mom. But here's another thing: I stumble every single day in motherhood. I yell. I pull my hair out. I hide in closets (yes, I do). I forget to feed my kids. I wonder what on earth I'm doing. I turn on the tv. I say yes to the

20th popsicle. I slump over in exhaustion. I forget to brush my teeth. I forget to brush my kids' teeth. I wonder how on earth I was given these three little miracles to guide through life. I mean, seriously, they look to me for everything. And what do I know?

So right now I'm putting two of them to bed. I brought a glass of white wine with me. My sister snuck in and handed me a glass of red. I didn't decline. This motherhood gig asks everything from us and then a bit more. No one has it all together, not even that mom on Instagram who looks so perfect. She was wiping poop out of her white sofa just a few minutes ago.

. . . .

We have a lot of moments throughout the day when we aren't our best versions of ourselves. But I think the point is that we're giving it our best shot, right? We're just doing the best that we know how to do. And it's ok if the world around us sees that. There's really no shame in letting those around us in on this little secret that we aren't flawless.

I imagine a world without flaws would be boring. Plus, allowing our stumbles to be seen helps everyone else around us feel better about their stumbles. Showing our imperfections, vulnerabilities, moments of weakness, missteps, whatever you want to call them, lets our kids know it's ok for them to do the same.

We force ourselves to hold our heads up high, slap smiles on our faces and pretend everything is 100% completely amazing all of the time. But it's hard. This is hard, and there's no shame in admitting that.

If we put up a facade of perfection, our children are learning that anything less (anything REAL) is not good enough. They don't need to grow up with that message. Let them see you stumble. Then let them see you pick yourself up and keep going.

One day I was walking home after dropping my son off at school. It's a steep hill and my two littles like to be smushed up against me as much as they possibly can. So I had the baby in the carrier and my daughter on my hip. I spend so much of my life like this. I can cook dinner like this. I can grocery shop like this. I can tell witty jokes while putting on my shoes while drinking coffee like this. So I'm basically a pack mule, and that's fine. Whatever. It is what it is.

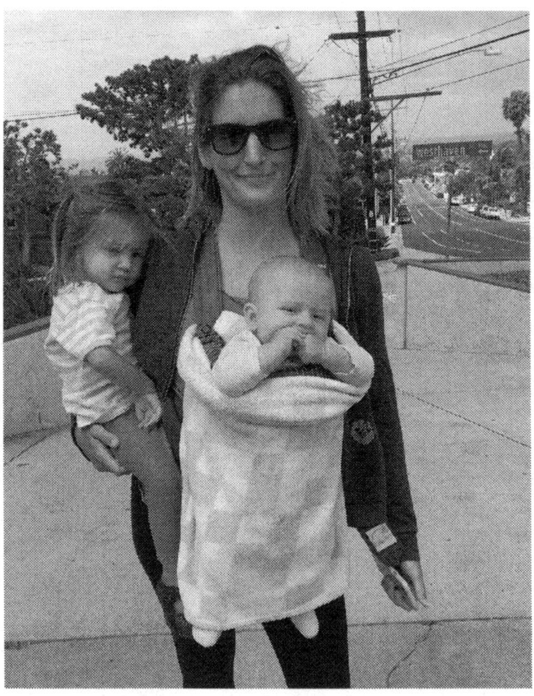

But on that day, a woman pulled over to the side of the road right in front of us. She threw her car in park, opened her door and jumped out. "Oh my! Do you need help? Is everything ok?! Can I help you?"

I was very confused. This was all very bizarre to me. Was she insane? Did SHE need help? So I asked her if she was talking to me. She was. So I asked her if I looked like I needed help. She said I did.

     Treading Water, Holding Weights

"Oh, no. I'm fine." I said. "We're fine. We do this walk all the time." She got in her car and drove away.

I mean, what a kind and sweet woman. I'm glad there are people around me, complete strangers, who will stop whatever they're doing to offer a hand. But her offer of help made me realize that this is me. This is my life right now. I stop traffic. Literally.

And so I thought 'Well, I'm not fooling anybody. If a woman driving by feels compelled to pull over, hop out and save me, surely there are more of these kind-hearted souls out there and surely I'm not fooling any of them with my sort of brushed hair, messy attempt at mascara and plastered-on smile. No. I'm not.'

Everyone has their struggle in life. Some struggles seem massive and some seem tiny, but to each of us, our struggles are very real and very hard. The world has a great way of telling us that we shouldn't show our struggles though. It's easy to see the neighbor's perfect yard or your friend's fabulous hair or the mom at library story time who is eight months pregnant and wearing a mini skirt with super cute hair and make-up on point and a freaking pedicure that definitely just got done and doesn't have a single chip and also her three year old is perfectly dressed and has adorable pigtails and my three year old won't keep her shirt on and hasn't worn shoes in two days and I can't get a brush close to her head and...hold on.

The point is that it's easy to look at the next person and see perfection. Seeing what we think is perfection in others has a sneaky way of making us more critical of ourselves, doesn't it? But I bet you perfection isn't there. Unless, of course, you change your definition of perfection, unless perfection includes a lot of messiness and chaos. Then perfection is attainable. In fact, you've probably already got it. Congrats. You're perfect. You can move on to your next mountain in life.

Seeing what we think is perfection in others has a sneaky way of making us more critical of ourselves, doesn't it?

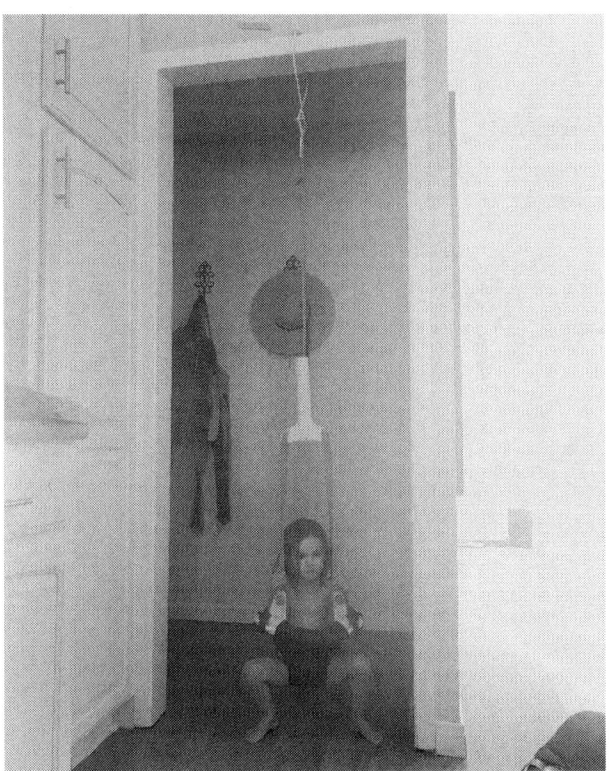

Miela refuses to get out of the baby's jumper. But she really doesn't fit in it any-more, and I'm quite positive she's going to rip out the entire door frame if she doesn't get over this obsession soon. She also growls at anyone who comes over and tells them, 'You can't come in here. You are bad.' It's a low, creepy voice, and I can't wait until this phase is over.

Isn't it funny how we wait and wait for our children to move out of phases? Do you know what's on the other side? Just another phase that'll drive us nuts.

Today Toren wanted to show me his 'six pack', but needed a flashlight to see it (naturally). He was sitting down, shining a flashlight at his stomach, and yelled that something was wrong. There was true panic in his voice. He explained that his six pack was gone and all he had was fat. I told him what happens to tummies when we sit down versus when we stand up. Then I showed him the difference on my stomach when I sat versus stood. 'No,' he plainly stated while I stood there exposing my stomach, 'you're still fat.' That little twerp.

I over-nursed Karoh on our flight home the other day. It was a rookie mistake. I still make those on baby #3. But it kept him quiet and helped with the elevation and all of that stuff. Unfortunately, ten minutes before we landed, he sat up and fire-hosed me three times with all of the milk and stomach acid in the world. My pants were absolutely soaking wet. My shirt was drenched. I smelled the worst. My hair... my hair. Three separate times. It couldn't be stopped and I just had to sit there and take it. I'd never seen anything like this in my life. The man across the aisle looked at me and said, 'Welp, there you go.' It was exactly what my dad would have said. I just nodded and held my head high.

Last night we went to the beach and the water was perfect and we all swam. 'Ah, life is good,' I thought. And it is. But then Miela threw up all over my face at bedtime.

This stuff. I couldn't make it up.

. . . .

Don't hesitate to curate your life. This is YOUR mind after all, and the world is full of a lot of beautiful stuff and a lot of horrible stuff. If you aren't the gate keeper of your mind, no one else will be. There are so many influences in the world waiting to get their message in front of you. Be picky.

Start with social media. Unfollow the accounts that don't make you feel better. Stop looking at the posts that don't fill you up. What are you looking for on social media? Start there! If something isn't getting you closer to that, let it go. Be picky, for crying out loud.

If you aren't the gate keeper of your mind, no one else will be.

Now, think about the other places you're going to fill yourself up. What are you reading? Who are you spending your time with? What are you talking about? When we find people who we really connect with, messages we resonate with and conversations that leave us feeling nourished, we have found that good stuff in life. Find more of those things. And I bet none of them will leave you wondering if you're enough or loved or raising your kids the right way.

I was talking with a good friend the other day about how we can teach our kids about eating healthy food. Of course we can force them to swallow that broccoli, but how do we get them to actually ASK for that broccoli. Now, I have a lot of thoughts on this topic, but the most interesting thing in our entire conversation came from my friend. She told me that she has taught her boys to pay attention to how they feel AFTER they eat that food. So after they eat Cheetos, how do they feel? After they eat an apple, how do they feel?

Your kids might say 'Mom, I feel great,' after eating the Cheetos, and that's ok. The point is that you're getting them to start to pay attention. You're asking them to notice the effects of what they're choosing to let into their bodies.

She uses the same approach with video games and TV. She asks them how they feel after they play a game or watch a show. The answer may not be shocking. Your kids may think you're crazy (you probably are), but at least you're planting the seed in their little brains that the decisions they make will affect how they feel. You're asking them to pay attention to those things, to be mindful of those things.

When we find people who we really connect with, messages we resonate with and conversations that leave us feeling nourished, we have found that good stuff in life.

So I'm asking you to do the same thing. You don't need to make any massive changes and certainly don't pass any judgement on yourself. But pay attention. After you scroll through Facebook, how do you feel? When you spend time online, are you getting from it what you want? After time with your friends or conversations with your closest circle, are you in a better place or not?

Obviously we don't expect to walk away from EVERY little event in life in a great mood. For example, the news. It's not always positive, but it's informative. If that's what you're looking for, it's not a bad thing.

Don't overthink it all, but DO think about it. Pay attention. Then begin to curate. You get to curate one life, and that's yours. So do it.

. . . .

INSTAGRAM POST JULY 20, 2018

Today I was en route from Cedarburg, WI back to my parents' farm in Madison. My little entourage and I made a stop to see one of my college friends. We were so close in college but haven't been able to see much of each other since then. She's a truly special soul. I've always known that.

My kids were tired. I was tired. We've been traveling for 3 weeks, just the kids and me. It's been so fun but also quite exhausting. I really had no clue how this pit stop would go. It could be all screaming and tears, or it could be smiles and laughs. But whatever. Here we go...

We walked in and I was handed a giant cold brew coffee. She took my baby from my arms and told me to relax. Breakfast sandwiches, muffins and hash browns were warm in the oven. Her three children welcomed my three children with play-doh, Pokémon cards and a little kitchen. We tried to catch up, but the kids made talking nearly impossible. But that was ok. We both totally understood this part of motherhood.

She said, 'Look, you can say no if you want...there's a yoga class at 10:30 at my club. We can drop the kids off at the kid center. The kids will play. I'll bring lots of snacks. You're traveling with three kids. I bet taking an hour to do something for yourself would be amazing.'

I was so caught off guard. I thought 'Oh, I can't do that. That's just crazy.' But then I realized that it WOULD feel amazing. And it did. It was so good.

I'd like to be that kind of person, the kind of person who sees someone else's struggle so clearly and knows exactly how to reach out to them. She swooped in, hugged me hard, lifted me up and sent me on my way a much more grounded and sane mama.

· ·

Find the people in your life who lift you up, and hold them closer. Find the people in your life who drag you down, and let them go. Or at least put some space between the two of you. There are a lot of opportunities in life for deep, nourishing, positive connection with people. Find more of that.

CHAPTER THREE

Put it on a Cloud: And teach this to your kids, too.

My niece was eight years old and someone at school was bothering her. I remember listening to her tell me all about it. It was really heavy for her. I couldn't help but think 'Oh, the world is going to throw this crap at you over and over again. Just walk right past it. Let it hit the sidewalk behind you and stay there.'

But advice like 'don't let it get to you' and 'just ignore it' doesn't really work for eight year olds. Does it actually work for any of us? Not really. I hate it when people say that stuff to me. I'm going through something and I'm telling you about it and I want you to FEEL it with me, not brush past it like it's nothing. It's something to me, dammit!

So I made up some genius advice on the spot, and it actually worked for her. Sometimes we surprise ourselves. Sometimes we do not, but SOMETIMES we do. This was one of those times.

I told her that things will happen to her all day long, both good and bad things. She is going to go through this every single day of her life. And SHE gets to choose how she lets those things affect the rest of her day. Now, if someone says something mean to her, she can hold on to it and feel bad about it. It can make her really unhappy for the rest of her day. She can give that thing and that person this power over her. OR, she can choose to put it on a cloud and let it drift away. Then she can continue on with her happy day. The cool thing is that SHE gets to decide.

People will say and do all sorts of things to us. All day long—this is life, people. But no one is making us feel a certain way. That's the part we get to decide on. And thank goodness, right? Can you imagine if the world got to decide how we felt every minute of our lives? How unpredictable would that be? And how devastating?

The cool thing is that my niece got it. She decided to put it on a cloud and then she felt better. I was like 'Hey, Melissa, nice one!'

Now, we could have gotten the kid's name and called the school and gone that route. Perhaps that's appropriate in some situations. But perhaps it's important to arm these kids with some tools to help them learn how to navigate the world on their own. After all, we won't always be there with our kids to help them learn how to handle tough situations. We can't go to the first day of college with them. We won't be by their sides at soccer practice. We won't go into their first day of work with them. So we might as well teach them how to understand tough situations when they arise so that they are confident, competent and capable (I didn't actually intend three "C" words, but it works) when they face the real world without us.

Can you even imagine them facing the big world WITHOUT US?! Yes, that day will come. Let's get them ready for it. That's our job.

And a few months later, my sister (my niece's mom) told me that my niece is still putting things on clouds. In fact, whenever she has a tough situation at school, they talk about whether or not she's going to put it on a cloud or hold on to it.

Sometimes you have to hold on to things. We can't toss everything into outer space and ignore it. But sometimes we don't need to carry things around with us. So let's release those things, and teach our kids to do the same.

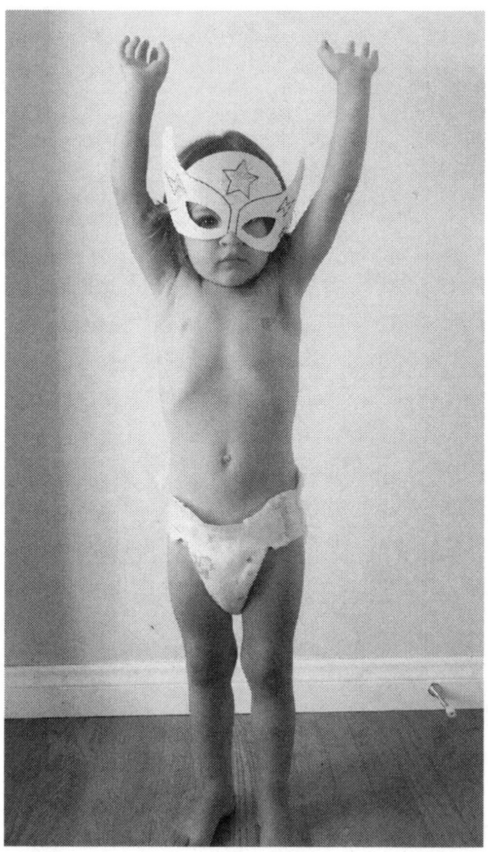

Miela is terrified of skeletons. She calls them pelicans.

Toren has spent the last three days trying to explain to her that she has a pelican in her body. It's very confusing. No one wants to accept that the thing they are most afraid of is actually INSIDE of them.

I found her hiding under a blanket this morning trying to figure out how to hide from the pelican inside of her. So instead of hiding, we decorated superhero masks, put on capes, blasted some music and ran around the house scaring away the pelicans and yelling 'I am brave and I am strong'.

Look, I don't always know what I'm doing here. I make it all up as I go. But I do know that putting on a superhero mask and cape makes you strong enough to take on anything in life, even the pelicans inside us. Also, Halloween is going to be a disaster with this one.

. . . .

Bringing kids into this world isn't easy in many ways. One of the scariest things is looking back at the road we have traveled to get where we are today and realizing they're going to have a long road to travel, too. We know so much more as adults. We have learned about the darkness in the world. We see the scary paths life can take, and we are terrified that our children may find themselves on one of those paths.

Locking them all in boxes seems like the only suitable answer to raising okay kids. But, we can't do that. There are laws against it, and aside from the laws, it's just not a good idea.

But it's so easy to want to shield them from all of the bumps in the road ahead. We just can't though. The bumps are an important part of it all.

I'd like other kids to be nice to my children. But I also think it's important that my children know what it's like when kids are mean to them, so they know why it's important to be nice to people.

I'd like school and sports to come easily for my kids, but I also want them to know what it's like to struggle at things, and to work hard at getting better. It's important that they know they aren't always going to be the best at everything. They aren't always going to win at everything. And that is perfectly fine.

I would love it if mental illness and anxiety and addiction and all of those tough things in life were never a factor for my children, but I also want them to know and understand these pieces of life. I want them to

. . . perhaps our greatest gift to them is to teach them to navigate the world and all of the ups and downs they will experience.

have compassion for those struggling, and I want them to know that they are not alone if they find themselves struggling one day.

So instead of protecting our children from life, perhaps our greatest gift to them is to teach them to navigate the world and all of the ups and downs they will experience. Perhaps it's also important for them to know we are here. No matter how tough it gets, we are here. We can't always solve the problem, but we are here and we can weather the entire storm with them. The storm can get ugly, but there are always sunny skies on the other side.

. . . .

INSTAGRAM POST NOVEMBER 30, 2018

Today they hit me with a triple tantrum. Have you ever had one of those? It's something else. All three of them, completely losing their minds, all at the same time. I scooped them all up. Well, most of them. And we made our way to the couch.

I just sat there and held them while they all lost their minds for five minutes. I'm ok going through the storm. Some things you can't go around, over or under, you just have to go through. Triple tantrums are one of those things. So we sat there.

Toren threw himself across my lap and yelled at me to let him go. I wasn't holding him. Miela yelled at me to hold her. I was already holding her. Toren screamed that he was hungry, then bored, then mad that I wasn't playing Uno with him. He wasn't hungry. I'm not sure about bored, but my job isn't to entertain him.

Miela threw herself at me like she was trying to knock out my teeth. Toren kicked. Miela rolled over my elbow. Toren told me that he wanted to go swimming, then build something, then read a book. I just couldn't keep up. Miela started doing this strange high pitched screaming thing that sounded like a goat being electrocuted. I asked her what that noise was and how she was possibly making it. So she kicked it into high gear and made that noise on repeat.

And Karoh, well, he wasn't crying for any reason other than that his brother and sister were crying, so he thought it was the right thing to do. But by the third kid, you can tell the fake cries from the real cries. He wasn't fooling me.

So I sat there looking out the window and thinking about a book I just finished. The book was pretty good, but the ending was predictable and that bummed me out.

And the kids, they all thrashed and hollered and yelled out all of the things they absolutely needed in that moment. I just held them, kept them from knocking each other out and considered a few other potential endings for that book I had just finished.

Eventually they stopped and I said 'Hey, who wants some pomegranate?' And the older two perked right up and said 'I do.' And that was it. Tantrums behind us, not to be spoken about again. Off to the pomegranates. Smiles and giggles.

Onward and upward.

. . . .

 TREADING WATER, HOLDING WEIGHTS

A day with children is a day filled with extremely high peaks and very low valleys. As the adult, the mom or the dad or whatever, it's kind of our job to try to remain a constant for them while they navigate the ups and downs. We can't travel to every peak and every valley with them. But we can hold them while they go there and be a safe landing pad when they return to middle ground.

CHAPTER FOUR

Accept Help: Stop saying "I'm ok." You may be. But you may not be.

I used to think saying "I need help" was showing weakness. I thought it was like admitting that I'm not good enough and I'm incapable of handling things. And you know what? It felt like the world was in agreement with me on this one.

I think I was always seen as a strong person growing up. My mom is a strong person. She raised six kids with a manic depressive husband on a small farm in Wisconsin. She kept us all going, got us to our 10 million activities, worked as a nurse, fed us, clothed us, took us on vacations, baked our birthday cakes from scratch, grew a fabulous garden and screamed like a psychopath at all of our soccer games. She worked hard. She was strong. She still is.

We don't see eye to eye on everything, but I always thought that was because we were so much alike. And I was happy to be like her. She was strong. And that's what I was supposed to be too, right?

But I'm not sure I really understood what being strong meant. I thought it meant I had to carry all of the weight on my shoulders, get everything done and never once accept help.

So that's how I started to live my life.

And it was exhausting.

And then I became a mother and it started to crush me.

"Can I get that door for you," someone would ask while I carried three grocery bags, a child in the baby carrier and another in a car seat in my other hand.

"Oh, no, I'm fine. I got it," I'd dismissively respond while I opened the door with my foot.

People would ask me how things were going. I'd respond with an exuberant "Great!" I just looooooved being a mom. I just looooooooved cleaning poop out of my carpet and trading my college degree for a culinary expertise in making snacks. Yeah, it was all great, every moment of it.

I felt like I couldn't tell anyone about the ways I was second-guessing every decision I made or the fact that I cried in the morning when I opened my eyes because I was too tired to get up for the day.

I worried that people would call me things like 'depressed' or 'dramatic' or even 'weak'. And that would be the end of me, the end of this persona I had spent years building up.

Motherhood was the end of that person though. It was motherhood that ended all of this for me. But it ended all of this for me in the most amazing way possible. I believe that motherhood can confine us and motherhood can define us. It can also liberate us and uncover so much depth that we never knew we had.

 Treading Water, Holding Weights

INSTAGRAM POST AUGUST 22, 2018

There's a lot happening here. While my neglected coffee cools behind me, I'm soothing a teething baby, playing Uno with a very competitive Toren, who talks a lot of trash, and teaching Miela her shapes and colors with flash cards.

All of the kids need all of the attention. My under-caffeinated brain is trying to figure out when and how I might possibly eat breakfast and perhaps get a drink of water. It's early. I'm scattered. Do I even have my contacts in?

Anton took this picture right before he left for work this morning. I looked at him and was a bit envious of his put together self, properly caffeinated and ready to head out into the adult world and do adult things, talk to adult people, think adult thoughts. But right before he left the house, he said, 'I'm sad. I don't want to leave you all. You guys look so happy.'

That grass. It's always greener on the other side. But I don't think I'm sitting in a field of green grass.

No. I'm sitting on an extremely steep slope of wild flowers. The wind is blowing in every direction and we're having an earthquake. But we have fun, laugh (and throw tantrums) a lot and the view is great.

. . . .

I started to realize that carrying everything on my shoulders and being everything to everyone was impossible. And trying to do this was crushing me and my family too.

Plus, have you ever noticed how much people LIKE helping you out? It's true. Helping someone else makes you feel really good about yourself, right? One day I realized that saying 'yes' to an offer for help wasn't actually the same as inconveniencing someone else. It was actually giving someone else the chance to feel good.

And then I realized that saying 'yes' to an offer for help wasn't actually admitting to the world that I was weak, depressed or dramatic. It was actually admitting that I could use a hand, and everyone could use a hand at some point. So why do we refuse to accept a helping hand? Why are we so quick to say 'No thanks, I got it,' and 'Oh no, I'm fine,' and 'No, no, no, I don't need help. I'm perfectly capable of carrying these three children, pushing this empty stroller, holding my hot cup of coffee, carrying this bag of sand toys and crossing this busy street on my own'?

Sometimes, we have to decide to choose "ease" instead of being stubborn. Once we do, the world starts to shift.

Sometimes, we have to decide to choose "ease" instead of being stubborn. Once we do, the world starts to shift.

     TREADING WATER, HOLDING WEIGHTS

ARCHIVED BLOG POST AUGUST 3, 2016

Today I went to my first yoga class after having baby #2. It was a challenging vin-yasa class and it felt amazing—hard but amazing. The teacher had us repeat 'I choose ease' to ourselves while we started class in child's pose. Sure, that was an easy one to say in my head while in child's pose, but it felt much different when I was holding plank with one leg lifted in the air. In that moment, it sounded more like a question than a statement: 'I choose ease?'

Was I really choosing ease in that moment? Am I actually choosing ease in life? Is it really that easy just to *choose* it?

I just had a baby. My threenager has as much energy as a tornado and he is a mon-ster at bedtime. I see the familiar lines of sleep deprivation creeping in when I look in the mirror. *Ah yes my friend, I remember you.*

I have been told that I seem to have this mom thing 'figured out'. I've also been told I'm doing it wrong. Many times. It's easier with baby #2, but I still question so much about so many things all the time. We take these little beings home from the hospital and we're supposed to know what to do with them? Really?

There are days when nothing seems easy. There are hours when I live far from ease. There are moments when I can't even figure out how choosing ease is an option.

Yesterday, I did something I never would have done when my first child was seven weeks old. I was too anxious, too high strung with baby #1. Yesterday I left my kids with my mom and went to get acupuncture. It felt so good. So this morning I left the kids with my mom *again* and I went to a yoga class. I haven't taken a yoga class in ages. And it felt so good. Tomorrow I'm thinking about going on a run. I bet it'll feel good, too.

So I'm giving this ease thing a shot. I'm choosing ease. Even when life is busy and tiring and taxing, I'm choosing ease.

Today I made myself a cup of tea, and it felt like ease. I took a nap with my baby instead of folding laundry, and it felt like ease. My toddler said 'stupid' and then looked at me waiting for a reaction. I ignored him and it felt like ease.

Life isn't always smooth right now. Babies cry and threenagers scream and to-do lists get so long. But that's all ok. I think I'm going to embrace this notion of 'ease'. I'm just going to roll with it and choose it and perhaps it really is that easy.

. . . .

Here it is: Accepting help may be hard at first. It may feel kind of uncomfortable and you may find that you're self-conscious about it.

But do it anyway.

Then do it again and again.

Suddenly life feels a little lighter and the world around you feels a bit warmer. You might meet your neighbors while they close your car door for you. You might get to know the guy who works at the grocery store while he pushes your cart out to your car. You could find a best friend in one of the other moms at school drop-off whose children are older and who lends a hand when your toddler pours your purse out in the grass and scatters your tampons, stash of diapers and wipes, and the contents of your wallet everywhere.

The world gets warmer when we smile back at that person who offered a hand and say, 'You can absolutely help me. Thank you.'

Accepting help may be hard at first. . . .
But do it anyway.

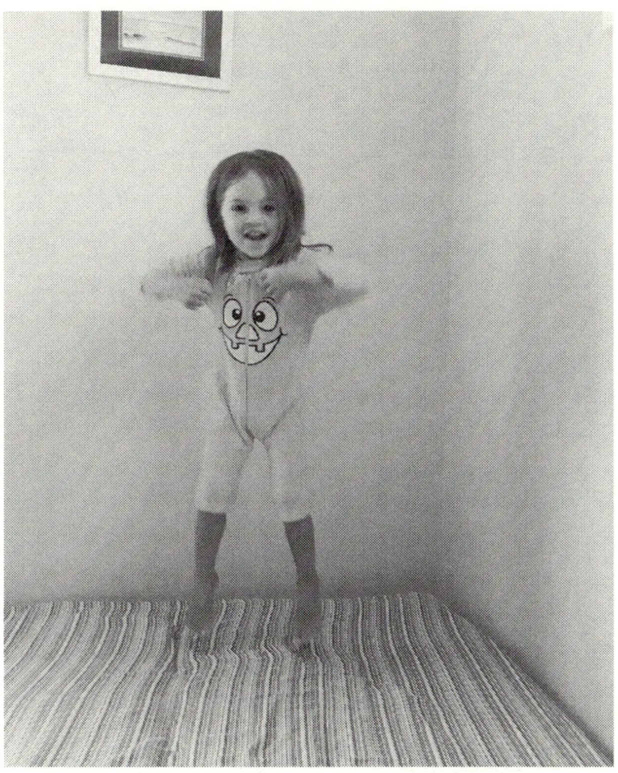

Well. She's going to be a pumpkin for Halloween. That was supposed to be Karoh's costume, but she has made it very clear that it's now hers. It's a size 6–12mos. She's two.

This morning I spent a very long time sitting on the floor having races between a two minute glass sand timer and the timer on my iPhone. We're all kind of sick and it felt like we were crawling through the morning two minutes at a time. I mean, I guess we were.

I'm a stay at home mom mostly and I still have someone come to the house two mornings a week. This brings me tremendous guilt. Somehow my mom managed with six kids. Shouldn't three be easy? It's not. It's the hardest thing I've ever done.

I say we are only going to watch tv on Fridays. I say no tv in the morning. I say we'll reserve tv only for special occasions or when I desperately need a break. I desperately need a break a lot lately. I think my kids are burning through all of Netflix.

I have a college education and good experience. My biggest achievement last week was filling out a volunteer application for my son's school and building a boat out of popsicle sticks. The boat lasted three minutes in water.

I volunteered at my son's school this morning (win) and the younger two cried the entire time I was away (loss). The mom guilt was so heavy.

Some days I look at myself in the mirror and think, 'Oh man, you're getting old.' Some days I look at myself in the mirror and think, 'Yikes! You look rough!' Some days I look at myself in the mirror and think, 'Hey! Are you still in there?'

My husband and I were talking about how hard life is with three littles. I told him I'm drowning some days. He said that was weird because I'm always telling him how happy I am and how I'm doing exactly what I want to be doing with my life. Here's the thing: he's right. That is how I feel. I'm confused by this. But it's true.

And still, I'm drowning.

Since I've been sharing a lot about mom life on social media, I've had a lot of people reach out to me. Some I know. Some I haven't seen in years. Some I've never met. Many tell me they resonate with my stories about the guilt, heaviness and madness of motherhood. Some share their own stories. Some say things like 'enjoy every moment' or 'cherish it all' or 'don't miss a second'. I think this last group of people are aliens.

I really am a very happy person and I really do love being a mom. It's awesome. But there's something very liberating in being able to say that it is very hard and it drives me nuts sometimes.

. . . .

 Treading Water, Holding Weights

Motherhood is glorious. It's fulfilling and redefines us as women. It gives new meaning to life and shows us that we are capable of far more than we ever thought possible. But it is a lot.

And we're all supermoms. Think of the amazing physical, emotional and mental hoops you've been through in motherhood? We're all supermoms.

Supermoms come in all shapes and sizes. Supermoms come in so many different versions and they show up in many different ways.

A supermom may be the one putting a career on hold to stay home with her children or the one dropping her kids off at daycare to rush off to work. She may be the one pursuing her own passions or putting her interests on hold to keep the house going. A supermom might make dinner at night or answer the door for delivery. She might co-sleep or sleep train or drink a lot of coffee to get through a long afternoon or hire a sitter so she can take a nap. You might bump into a supermom at the grocery store or at the library, maybe at the nail salon or in spin class.

Sometimes motherhood feels really good and sometimes it feels really hard, and that's fine. We're still all super at this and that's one thing we don't need to question.

Supermoms come in so many different versions and they show up in many different ways.

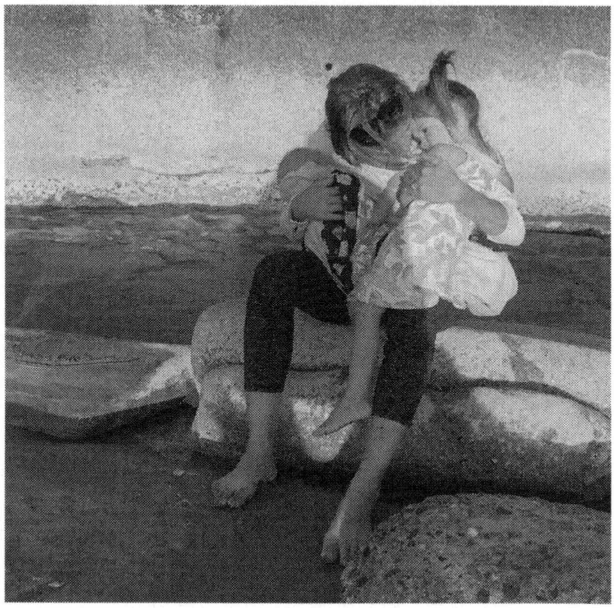

The sun is setting. We're at the beach. We've all been playing in the tide pools at low tide. Everyone is wet and getting tired and hungry. So everyone needs mom. We have a long walk back to the car.

I'm pretty sure that mothers have this magical ability to become Home. Wherever they are, they instantly become Home when the kids need it. Sometimes it means holding more children than you thought your arms could hold, sandy kids piling into your lap, everyone needing something immediately. But that soothing voice, that strong embrace, the reassurance that everything is ok, that's what mom is. That's what Home is.

My mom becomes Home in an instant. And I remember it well from when I was young. I never imagined that I'd become Home too. But here I am on a rock at the beach, snuggled in my children's bed in the middle of the night, picking my son up from school, reading books on the couch, riding on an airplane, nursing a hurt knee.

Suddenly I'm Home.

CHAPTER FIVE

See the Amazing: Yes, it's there!

On top of the chaos, the struggles, the constant mom guilt and the cries for help, this motherhood gig is pretty awesome. The way our hearts keep growing and growing, the way we find we have so much more to give, the new pieces of ourselves that emerge when we become mothers, it's all awesome.

And these little kids, they bring a ton of beauty into our lives, more than we could have imagined. There's no denying that. But if we aren't careful, we can miss it. We can let it slip right past us. If we don't slow down and pay attention, we just might miss the most amazing parts of motherhood.

For the first two years of my first child's life, I was working full-time. I remember my mornings were so hectic. Trying to get myself ready while also getting my son ready so we could get out of the house on time and in a mildly presentable fashion was no small feat. All working moms know this struggle.

If we don't slow down and pay attention, we just might miss the most amazing parts of motherhood.

He was an early riser. He was up by 5am. For a while, I fought this. I tried tirelessly to get him to sleep longer, I shifted his bedtime schedule, added more activities, fed him later. I tried it all. His body wanted to get going at 5am. So my body had to do the same, and I was not happy about it. These early mornings were painful.

Finally, I decided that perhaps he wasn't the one who needed to shift.

Perhaps it was me.

So I started going to bed earlier so that I would be a better version of myself when 5am rolled around. I planned an hour activity in the morning for us to do before we had to start getting ready for our day at 6am. I bought finger paints, window markers and chalk. Every morning at 5am, we rolled out of bed and had art time. It was glorious painting the floor to ceiling windows of our 6th story apartment while the sun came up over the eucalyptus trees. Some days we traded in our art supplies and built enormous forts that would take over the entire living room. Then there were the days where we built entire towns out of blocks, towns that spread across the coffee table and onto the bookcase.

It was so much fun. It was way better than being grumpy about getting up early.

I almost missed those moments, those glorious early mornings. I fought hard to find a way around them, but, thankfully, I lost that battle and the early mornings came day after day. It was great bonding time for us. After all, at 8am I dropped him off at school and then made my way to work. We were apart for a lot of the day. So it was precious to be able to spend those early mornings together being creative and having fun.

Kids are lucky. They get things like play time and story time. They get to make messes and explore. They run freely and swing and jump. Kids make art with abandon and laugh wildly so many times a day. They love being tickled and they are fascinated by mud. These are all great things.

Perhaps these are things we could use a bit more of in our lives? When's the last time you hung upside down from a tree or stepped in paint and then walked across a blank piece of paper?

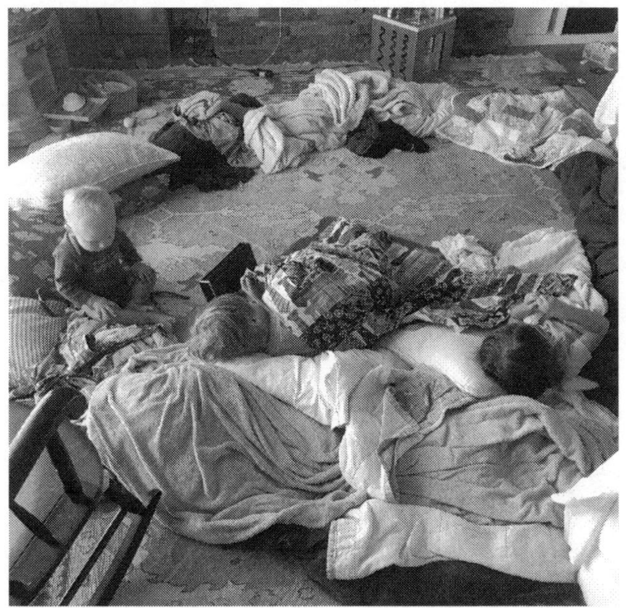

My kids like to make nests. A nest is basically a circle of blankets, pillows and any-thing else they can collect from around the house. They spend long periods of time lounging in these nests, listening to podcasts, readings books, etc. And they all just kind of stay in the nest for a really long time. There's some unspoken rule that no one leaves the nest.

I clear out all choking hazards and then sneak away, only popping up to deliver snacks and perhaps find a new podcast or pass along some new books. I keep a very low profile. My job is to keep the peace within the nest without drawing any attention to myself.

Though the nest walls are low, they'll stay in there as long as it's all smooth sailing. But when things turn sour within the nest, it goes downhill quickly, and my job is to evacuate everyone while they're still in one piece.

Today, they were in the nest, and Toren informed Miela that she wasn't big enough to do something. She replied 'I am bigger.' He responded 'Miela, what does bigger mean.' She spat out 'It means that you shut up.'

There was a part of me that really appreciated this response.

But then things got ugly and the nest was abandoned. It was good while it lasted. We'll try again tomorrow.

Also, I want a nest. They're cozy, warm, relaxing and there's some invisible wall there that seems to separate the nest inhabitants from the outside world. I want to spend the day in a nest.

But for now, I'm just the nest food delivery gal trying to find a way in.

. . . .

Childhood comes with this amazing ability to explore the imagination without being worried about how it will be interpreted by the outside world. Kids do amazing things and play amazing games. They sing loudly and move freely. At some point, we grow older and we dampen this freedom. We quiet these precious pieces of ourselves. But why?

It wasn't until I became a mother that I began to remember how I used to experience life as a child.

The first time I took my son to story time at the library, I was in shock. We all sat around in a circle while the sweet librarian sang songs and read stories. It was soothing and entertaining.

Now, I wasn't exactly in the easiest phase of my life at this point. I was exhausted and stressed out. I spent my days chasing a toddler who never ever stopped moving and I was certain I was doing everything wrong. I struggled to find peace and stillness in my life, but I was a yoga teacher, and peace and stillness was something I craved.

It wasn't until I became a mother that I began to remember how I used to experience life as a child.

     TREADING WATER, HOLDING WEIGHTS

So this story time thing, it was novel. I just sat there, and my son did too. The librarian read a few books. No one had read me a book in a long time. I was usually the one reading the books. Have you ever noticed that when you're the one reading the book out loud, you barely have time to look at the pictures? You may give them a glance, but you kind of skip past them and on to the next page. You're missing one of the glorious parts of children's books!

But sitting there, listening to the story, looking at the pictures, it was amazing. I looked around at all of the other tired moms around me and thought, 'This is exactly what we need! This is brilliant.'

Then I thought of my husband. This was exactly what he needed too! I was sure of it. He would love it.

Then I thought of all of the hurried, stressed out, tired people running around out there and thought 'Everyone needs library story time. It's soothing, relaxing, slow and so sweet.' From there, my little brain started thinking about all of the amazing things I was now doing with my child that I never did before becoming a mother, or at least I hadn't done these things in decades, since I was a child myself.

Finger painting is very therapeutic and satisfying. Slow walks in the park where you don't cover much ground but you look at everything in detail, those walks are fascinating and relaxing. Running without any particular destination, just to see how fast you can move your feet, it's freeing.

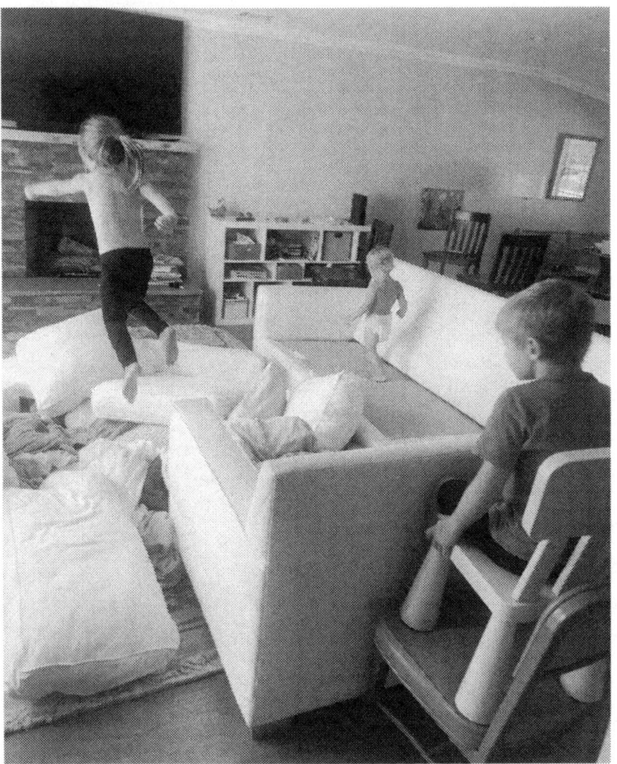

Climbing Cabunga

My kids play a game called Climbing Cabunga. It's their favorite and my least favor-ite. They take off all of the couch cushions, strip all of the pillows and blankets off of the beds and throw everything in the middle of the living room.

Then they rearrange the furniture and jump off of everything into the massive pile. It sounds somewhat harmless. It sounds like something I certainly did when I was little. The terrifying thing is that the floor is hard and the placement of the cushions is suspect. There is a stone fireplace with sharp corners and a floor to ceiling window.

My oldest son stacks one chair on top of another and perches up there. He says he's the lifeguard. That brings me just a little solace, but mostly more anxiety. The one year old bounces around the place. The three year old jumps from the top of the couch. My six year old screams at them and tells them they're out of bounds, whatever that means. It's lifeguard speak.

All of this is horrible and terrifying. But last week during a particularly intense session of Climbing Cabunga, I made an entire lasagna. So, I'm not sure what to do here. I am very torn.

The truth about parenting is that nothing gets done when the children are playing quietly together, because that is not something that ever happens. They only want 100% to be dangerous and fight.

If you can find a happy medium and let them be just a tad dangerous, but not fight at all, then you've found a sweet spot. There's no fun in childhood in the safe zone. Something exciting happens in the danger zone. The mildly questionable games are the ones that keep everyone happy and engaged for hours.

Now, I'm not condoning dangerous situations for our children. Certainly not. I'm just saying that that's when lasagnas are made.

. . . .

There are a lot of things that we get to revisit when we have children, things we haven't even thought about since we were young. But as adults, we have different expectations and an entirely new set of activities that are considered appropriate for this phase of our lives. And sometimes the slow pace, the curiosity and excitement that children put into exploring a small patch of grass on the side of a dirty, busy street, sometimes this drives us mad.

We don't have time to stop and look at that leaf. It's probably filthy and it's just a leaf and we've seen a million leaves before and there are people everywhere and we can't just stop here and we have to get to the grocery store immediately and we have to get going and can you hurry up?

But, usually, we can stop and look at that leaf and we SHOULD stop and look at that leaf, even if it looks ordinary and boring at first glance.

My point here is that being a parent gives you another chance to experience the amazing pieces of childhood that most adults have forgotten about. But we have to see these opportunities when they pop up, otherwise they come and go before we realize it. We have to shift our expectations so that we can thoroughly enjoy these moments again.

So don't miss the amazing. You aren't too busy or too cool or too much of an adult.

. . . .

INSTAGRAM POST AUGUST 2, 2018

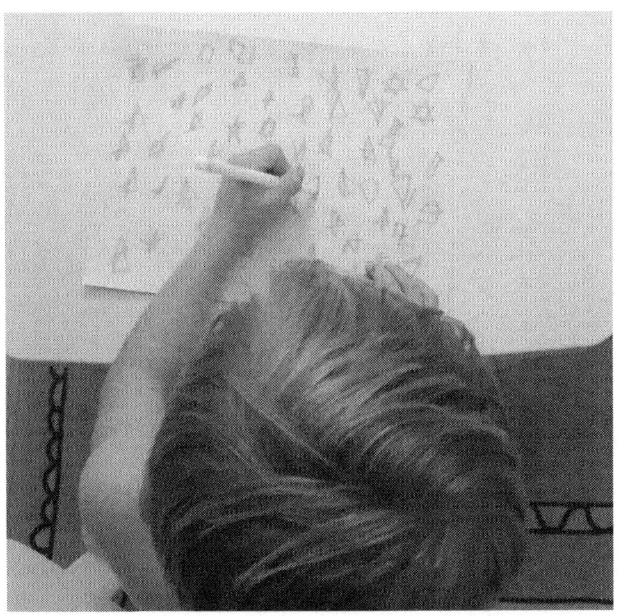

Learning to make stars. All of these things we know how to do, we had to learn them at some point. All of them. Watching my kids learn everything, especially the things that seem simple, takes a lot of patience. I could jump in and make the stars for him. I could tell him to move on and that he'll learn to make them at some point later on. I could tell him we have to get to the grocery store or whatever else seems so pressing. But this is the important stuff. Persistence. Focus. Determination. Making stars. I think it's in these little moments that our children are building important muscles.

CHAPTER SIX

Slow the Eff Down: This isn't a race. You die at the finish line.

Look, I know that sometimes (or maybe it feels like ALL of the time) we find ourselves counting the hours until bedtime. We look at the clock and think 'ok, just three more hours until the day is done and I can sleep.' And, hey, that's ok. I mean, these days can be really tough and seemingly endless. But if we find ourselves falling into this pattern EVERY day, then perhaps it's time to make some shifts.

After all, the finish line of life isn't exactly a finish line we want to race towards.

I've heard many times that the days are long, but the years are short. After so many people have said this to me, I suppose there must be truth there. But the truth for me, and possibly for you too, is that when my days start at 4am with a child screaming for me and end at 9pm with a child screaming for me, these days can feel long and brutal. There's not enough space in my head to think about what the years are feeling like.

I know. You know. Some of these moments can feel heavy.

So this past year I made a promise to myself that I would be more mindful in motherhood and take a deep look at what exactly it was that was making these days feel long and painful. Of course, not every moment was painful. There were gloriously beautiful moments in there too. Many of them. But I found myself thoroughly exhausted by motherhood, and the heavy moments were coming up for me far more often than I wanted. And when motherhood feels heavy and the days start to drag on, my least favorite version of myself starts to come out. No one wants that! I call this version of myself the Mommy Monster. The Mommy Monster has no patience, a horrible scowl and a very terrifying yelling voice. She comes out every now and then, but I do what I can to keep her at bay.

Do you want to know what I realized during this past year of paying attention to these moments in motherhood? I realized that the hardest times for me were the moments when the reality of my situation was not matching up with my expectations for what it should be like.

With three little kids ages six and under, and one more on the way, can you imagine how often I found my expectations not matching up with the reality of my situation? Quite often. (I actually mean almost ALL THE TIME, but I'm too ashamed to say that, of course. After all, admitting to that would be admitting that I'm not completely on top of everything, all the time.)

It took me a few years of motherhood to realize that many of my struggles came about because I wasn't quite able to loosen up my expectations. I had not yet realized that things need to seriously change now that small, unpredictable human beings were a part of the equation.

But once I did, things went more smoothly. The main thing was slowing down. My pace has always been quick. I multi-task and jump from one thing to the next. I'm always on the go and rarely idle. In college, I'd start the day with soccer practice at 6am, then take off for classes from 8am–noon. Next I'd book it to the gym to get my endurance and strength training in, run back to classes and then sprint to work to finish off the day. I'd leave my house at 5:30am and not return until after 9pm. It was quite normal for me and became the pace of life I thought I thrived in.

That's not how kids are. They don't function that way and disaster happens when we try to make them. Kids need their snuggles in the morning, before we jump into the day ahead of us. They need our undivided attention when they show us their latest discovery. They need us to listen fully while they explain their dreams to us, circling around and around and starting over seven times before they get distracted by a pair of sunglasses and walk away without finishing the riveting tale.

This isn't easy for adults. The problem is, kids know when they have half of our attention. They know when we're trying to do the dishes, check our email, listen to a podcast AND convince them that they have our full

　　　　　　　　　TREADING WATER, HOLDING WEIGHTS

We create a chaotic, busy grind if we aren't careful. And when we try to merge children into this frantic pace, we set ourselves up for disappointment and frustration.

attention while they tell us about their latest drawing of a cat in a canoe stuck up in a tree. They are on to us.

So slow down. Maybe even STOP. Turn off the water, put your phone down, take out your ear buds and get down to their level. Ask them about that cat and find out how it got in that canoe and let them tell you why that ridiculous canoe is up in that tree.

It's hard. At least at first. But it's worth it.

See, our society tells us that we have to accomplish more and check everything off our to-do lists. Actually, we fill up our to-do lists endlessly without giving ourselves an actual shot at ever completing it all. And when we find an idle moment with nothing to do, we pull out our phones and fill our minds with the endless abyss of social media or we check email one more time or we see what on earth Quora has to say about anything at all.

We create a chaotic, busy grind if we aren't careful. And when we try to merge children into this frantic pace, we set ourselves up for disappointment and frustration. Also, we miss some of the most amazing moments life has to offer.

Kids don't tie their shoes quickly. They eat a little more slowly. They find their surroundings interesting and can be easily distracted. They want to explore and move slowly through their days. But we don't always leave space and time for that. Perhaps we need to.

And what are we racing towards anyways? The finish line of life isn't exactly a target I'm rushing towards. But it's so easy to tell yourself that things will get better once this day is over, when this month ends, when you child is out of this phase, once they learn to do something. We say that things won't be as hard when we finally achieve this or do that or move on from whatever it is that's slowing us down.

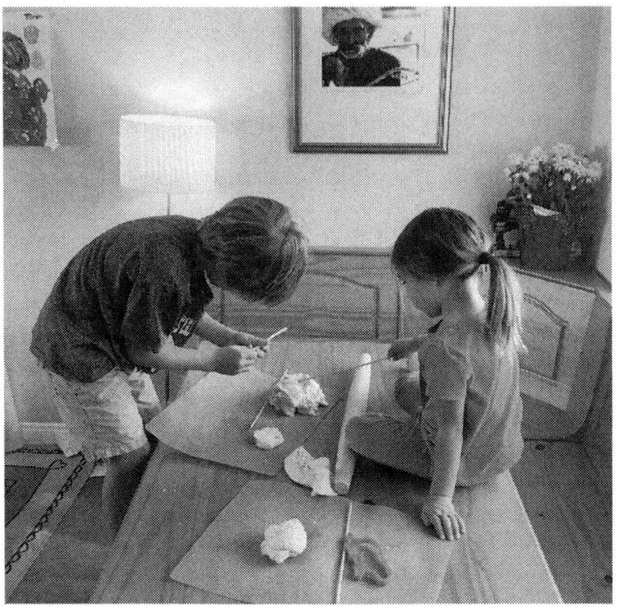

Mama, Make a Zig Zag Square

Christmas is around the corner. It's that time of year. I'm not really that good at this stuff, this holiday fancy. Now, I'm not a scrooge. The holidays are fabulous in many ways and I rise to the occasion when the big day rolls around. However, I don't really decorate and I buy presents last minute and we don't bake cookies.

But today, today I must have had an extra cup of coffee in the morning. I decided that we were going to make our own ornaments, the kind where you have to make the dough, roll it out, cut the ornaments, bake them, paint them and hang them. We got to work, my little crew and I.

We mixed the dough and kneaded it with those tiny hands. Flour took over the kitchen and I held my tongue while it ended up in everyone's hair. Some things you just have to let go, and flour in hair is one of them. We have one cookie cutter. That's right, one. I thought it was a bear, but as we were using that one cookie cutter in the dough, I realized it made more of a cheetah.

We cut out cheetah after cheetah after cheetah. In an effort to avoid a Christmas tree filled with Christmas cheetahs, I decided to cut out a few shapes. I started with circles and then got creative and jumped over to squares, which can easily be turned into diamonds. So we have diamonds too, a few triangles and even an oval.

My 5 year old admired my circle cutting and I thought, 'yes, my circle is spot on. Point mom.'

But after sweetening me up with a compliment, he quickly turned on me. "Mom," he started, "make a fish." Well, I can make circles, really good circles. Surely I can figure out a fish.

My first attempt failed, but my second was quite good. My son was satisfied and I jumped back to making cheetahs. "Mom," he continued, "Make a zig zag square." Now what the hell? I turned to look at him, swallowed hard. "A zig zag square?" I questioned. "Yes," he replied, staring at me. Ok, I can do this. I've got it. A zig zag square. A...what the hell? Ok, here we go.

"Ok," I stated while slowly nodding my head, adamant to show no weakness. The challenge had been tossed out, and the challenge had been accepted. I gave him no hint that I was clueless, that I didn't know what a zig zag square could possibly be. Surely it's nothing, right? Just something a child made up, right? But it's something to him, so it will be made.

I hesitated for a moment. "You know," he went on, "with the castle line." Oh yes, sure kid. The "castle line". "Mmm" I said, not exactly a "yes" and not exactly a "no". And so I started and he watched, intently. I cut lines and squares and some-how made them all join together and more lines and some shapes and eventually, something emerged.

I put my knife down. I didn't look at him.

He got a bit closer, staring at my zig zag square. "There. [swallowing hard] A zig zag square," I said, sounding very confident. Too confident. "Is that a zig zag square?" he asked. "It is," I replied. "That's the castle line?" he asked. "Yes, that is," I said boldly.

He looked at me and I dared to look back. I knew that if I let him see any weakness, any uncertainty, any wavering at all, he would tell me that was NOT a zig zag square and that my castle line was all wrong and that I needed to start all over. There may be tears.

The younger two were getting close to nap time and any show would definitely cascade down to them, erupting into a chaotic frenzy of tears and tantrums and more needs than I could fulfill. I was running on an empty stomach and couldn't quite navigate a triple tantrum.

He slowly nodded, not 100% buying it, but not able to come up with a sound argument. I had won. Or had I? "Ok," he said back to me, "ok, now make a zig zag fish."

I braced myself for the triple tantrum.

. . . .

The honest truth is that once our kids are out of this one phase, they'll be in another. Once they're sleeping through the night, they'll start teething or throwing tantrums or running away from you in public. Once this day is over, there will be another and then yet another, if we're lucky. Once we achieve this one thing, we'll move on and set our sights on something else we think we need to achieve in order to be happy and feel at peace.

I believe that the thing we're after in life is progress. I can't actually take credit for figuring this one out though. I worked for years for Tony Robbins in his marketing department. One of the huge bonuses of working for this man was that I got to go through all of his products and attend all of his live events. Hey, if I was going to market them all, I had to see them through the eyes of one of his clients. It was a pretty good job perk, and it changed my life completely.

I remember sitting in one of the front rows at one of his huge events, looking up at this enormous man on stage. He was talking about what true happiness was all about.

This was a topic I was tremendously interested in because for years I'd felt unsatisfied with where I was in life. I felt like I'd make a goal, achieve it and still find myself unhappy. I couldn't figure out what I was doing wrong

    TREADING WATER, HOLDING WEIGHTS

or what would truly make me happy. I was frustrated with my constant searching and searching.

But then he said something that clicked on a lightbulb in my head. He told us that the secret to happiness is PROGRESS and that reaching a goal is only satisfying temporarily. Ah, yes! That made complete sense. It wasn't the actual achievement that was giving me happiness. It was the work I put in to achieve it. I found the progress satisfying, not the end goal.

At this point in my life, I was not yet a mother. But now that I am a mother, I often find myself remembering this important life lesson and applying it to my life with my children.

I remember years ago when my husband and I were on a walk in Balboa Park with our oldest, who was two at the time. Before we set off on this walk, I had a destination in mind. We would make it all the way to the fountain in the park, turn around and then walk home. The distance was ambitious for a two year old, but it was the walk I had in mind, so it was what we were going to do.

As soon as we hit the park, my son started perusing the grass, strolling around trees on repeat and running up and down this small hill at the edge of the park. I grabbed his hand and started pulling him along. He fought back. I asked if my husband would pick him up. My husband just stared at me and said, "Let's just go at his pace. It's ok if we only cover 20 yards. This is what he wants to do."

And I was a little blown away. Wow! Yeah. He was right. Why was I so determined to get moving? This walk was essentially just a chance for us to spend time together, outside as a family. Who cared if we walked a mile or just 10 yards.

Then I started noticing all of the moments in my life as a mother where I was unnecessarily rushing things or somehow causing more chaos and stress when it completely wasn't necessary. See, I was used to accomplishing a lot, and fast. I was used to achieving one thing and moving right on to the next.

But I was missing the beauty in slowing down, moving at a child's pace and just enjoying the progress we were making, even if it felt like very little progress.

And what does "progress" mean anyways? Sure we weren't walking far, but we were exploring, feeling the grass between our toes and soaking in some sunshine. We were chatting, laughing and letting our son browse the world in his own way.

I think that's important progress in life. Right?

. . . .

INSTAGRAM POST DECEMBER 13, 2019

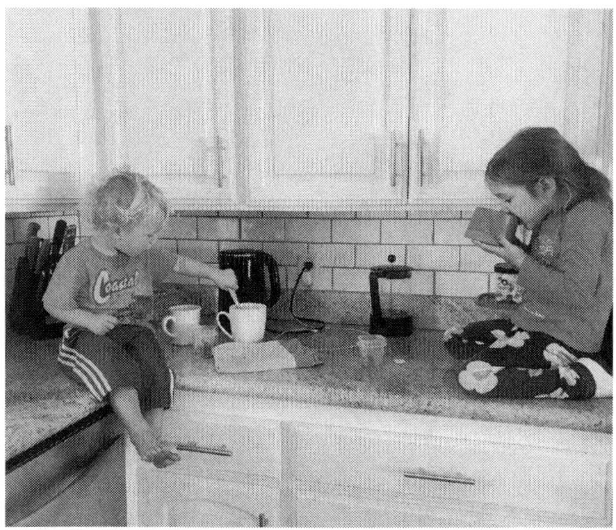

If you thought we were uncivilized barbarians over here, well, you're absolutely right.

But we are uncivilized barbarians who make time for tea…on the counter. Forget that my kids are all on the counter. Just ignore that for a moment. They basically live on my counters. The point here is that we make TIME FOR TEA. My children love it, and so do I.

They're 50% Russian, so that may have something to do with it. My husband and his family are tea maniacs. Completely wild about the stuff. And that appears to have been passed down to my kids.

So we pause the chaos. We put the brakes on jumping off of the furniture, riding bikes through the house and spitting at each other when we don't think mom is looking (I'm always looking), and we have tea. Peppermint, turmeric, ginger,

　　　　TREADING WATER, HOLDING WEIGHTS

licorice, anything. We love our tea. But once teatime is done, the chaos resumes 110%.

Karoh is figuring out the English language. He points to the sky when birds fly by and yells 'B*tches!' I can't bring myself to correct him. He did it at school drop-off yesterday and I just smiled and said 'That's right honey.' The crows in Carlsbad are super annoying, so he's not too far off.

Toren asked me 'Who is Jesus's dad, God or Zeus?' To which I replied with a long explanation that included the diversity of beliefs we have in our world. In the end, he concluded that it must be Zeus because Zeus was the god of gods.

Gramma Joan, this one has a lot of questions, so I'm going to have you take a deep dive into the religions of the world at Christmas time. This is your heads up.

We called my gramma GG. She passed away a few years ago. She was awesome. Miela confuses baby Jesus with baby GG. She thinks Christmas is all about baby GG's birthday and loves playing with our nativity set…which includes baby GG, of course. I am positive my gramma is looking down at me, rolling her eyes and saying 'Oh, Melissa!' Mom, maybe you can sort this one out when we're home for Christmas too?

. . . .

The beauty and the hilarity and all of the magnificence can be found in the strangest places in motherhood. Right? But we have to have a chance to notice it, and noticing things isn't very easy when we're going 100mph all the time.

The beauty and the hilarity and all of the magnificence can be found in the strangest places in motherhood.

So stop for a moment right now and take a step back from your experience as a mother. What is your pace? How does it feel? Where is it bumpy and where is it smooth?

Are there parts of life as a mom that you're unnecessarily speeding through? What are you giving up by rushing these moments?

And what does progress mean to you? How are you defining your success in motherhood? Is it in the accomplishments or the moments in between?

Give this some real thought. If we rush through it all, we're missing all of the good stuff while we're busy searching for what we THINK is the good stuff.

CHAPTER SEVEN

Remember Yourself: You're still there. A few wrinkles, a few grays, but it's you.

I entered motherhood fresh out of my 20s, ready to start a new decade of life. My hair was thick and shiny, the skin on my face was taut and clear, and I was just coming off of another marathon. My career was fulfilling, I practiced a lot of yoga and my brain was finally maturing, which meant that life was beginning to make a little more sense to me.

I was ready for a baby. My husband and I were ready. We could handle it.

And now I'm winding down my 30s, not even an entire decade later. I'm pregnant with my 4th child. I see new wrinkles setting in daily. I hate highlighting my hair, but the grays keep coming in stronger and stronger. I am up well before the sun (and my kids) a handful of days a week to work out, not because I am so thrilled to work out before most people have opened their eyes, but because I'm starting to see how quickly things catch up to me (mostly my thighs) if I don't maintain a strict and consistent regimen of high intensity training.

I have vowed to myself that yoga is going to find its way back into my life, as well as a career of some sort. But the truth is, I can't figure out how either could possibly fit into my days anymore. Where is there possibly time and space in this foggy brain of mine to take on the business world? And yoga, ah yoga. It shouldn't be so hard. I'm making excuses, I know I am. Don't be mad at me yoga, I'll come back to you. I will.

Have I ever told you about my onion theory? Well, here it is: I believe we're all like onions. We all have a bunch of layers and as we grow, more can be added. One layer might be your career, another your family and another your hobbies. Maybe you're an avid cyclist. That's another layer. Or perhaps you play the cello. That's a layer. You may have a spouse or partner layer. Or you may have a friendship layer. Basically, the layers are all the different parts of yourself, all of the pieces that make up your identity.

When I became a mother, I took on another layer. If you're a mom, you did too. And that's great. The thing is, I started to see my motherhood layer taking over all of the other layers. That motherhood layer started covering up all of the other layers completely, until it was the only layer I could see on my onion. I woke up one day feeling entirely confused and terrified.

Who exactly had I become and why was motherhood the only part of me I associated with anymore? There was so much more to me before, right?

It was a moment of panic.

I loved motherhood dearly, but it was suddenly becoming my entire identity. Being responsible for a little life is a tremendous responsibility, and I didn't want to put my baby's well-being on hold for my own pursuits. I wanted to give him everything, and that's exactly what I was doing. And I was completely losing myself in all of it.

Does any of this sound familiar?

This new and tremendous layer to the onion isn't always an easy thing to take on. Often stepping into motherhood comes with so much more than we ever could have imagined, and the pressure to do our absolute best at it is tremendous. The stakes are high! We all want to raise the best children that we can.

It should be an important goal of ours to maintain our own sense of identity outside of motherhood.

 TREADING WATER, HOLDING WEIGHTS

If we allow ourselves to stay healthy and find happiness, to tackle our dreams and stay true to who we are, we are giving them one of the greatest gifts—a role model.

But we don't have to lose ourselves in this process. In fact, we shouldn't. It should be an important goal of ours to maintain our own sense of identity outside of motherhood. At least I think so.

And here's why.

We are capable of so much on this planet. We are mothers, yes we are, but we are also so much more. There are a lot of layers to our onions, and we need to give those layers space and time to grow. When we do not do this, we begin to feel suffocated. We begin to harbor resentment and feel disappointment. These things start as small seeds within us, but they will grow. Plus, and perhaps even more important, there's far too much within you to ignore. If we hold back on the many gifts we have to offer this world, we miss the chance to contribute to everything and everyone around us in astounding ways.

Remember, we are raising tiny humans, and we want them to grow up, move out, stay healthy and find happiness. We want them to tackle their dreams and stay true to who they are. And that's exactly what our parents probably wanted for us. If we allow ourselves to stay healthy and find happiness, to tackle our dreams and stay true to who we are, we are giving them one of the greatest gifts—a role model.

On my quest to gather the pieces of myself outside of motherhood, I made the kids breakfast, kissed my husband goodbye and snuck out of the house this morning. I grabbed my yoga mat and headed for a snug little yoga studio in Carlsbad called Woven We Are. It felt like such an indulgence. I rarely do anything like this, ever. I used to, but those days feel like a lifetime ago.

This morning was a Sound Healing & Meditation class. No movement. No downward facing dogs. No tree pose. Just lying there on my back, listening to the super healing sounds and gently escorting thoughts out of my mind every time they tried to make an appearance.

There were no diapers, no snacks to make, no messes to clean up. Just so much peace and stillness.

Don't get me wrong, motherhood is an epic journey and I love it. But. But. But. Stepping away from it, man, it felt good. I'm still there, deep down, beneath the amazing layers of motherhood. There's still Melissa in there. Sometimes I can't find her and I fear she's lost forever. But she's there.

. . . .

You want to know how long the idea for this book has been growing in my brain? Years. It's been a little seed in my brain trying to sprout, then it started to sprout but I made a million excuses why I couldn't write it. And all of those excuses had to do with motherhood. But the book idea kept popping up in my brain, over and over again. It was something I knew I wanted to do, I knew I had to do, but I couldn't find a way to do it.

At least that's what I kept telling myself.

I was convinced that my children gave me all of the reasons in the world TO write, but at the same time they gave me all of the reasons in the world NOT TO write. They made me a mother and gave me all of the inspiration I needed to write endlessly about real, raw and uncensored motherhood. But they sucked everything out of me at the same time. They demanded all of my time and zapped up all of my energy. I couldn't begin to imagine how I could find the creative spark to write an entire book in between the chaos of motherhood.

But this passion of mine kept coming back. Do you have something like that in life? Something that you want to do, you must do, but motherhood seems to stand in your way?

Well here's what I did about it. I had been keeping this book dream a secret for quite some time. I was kind of embarrassed of it or scared of it or maybe even intimidated by it. But one day I decided to talk to my husband about it. He's incredibly type A and goes directly to the solution

Just do it. Find the time, a little every day.

of every problem. This isn't always what I want though. Sometimes it just feels good to have someone sit and listen to your problems, someone who will empathize with you and maybe even validate all of the bullshit excuses you've made up in your head. After all, I had created quite the story as to why I couldn't write this book. I had so many reasons and nearly all of them centered around motherhood, one of the absolute most important layers to my onion. It was hard for me to put anything in front of my mom duties, and writing a book certainly didn't seem to make the cut.

But when I'm looking for someone to empathize with me and to validate my bullshit excuses, I know that my husband is the absolute last person I should turn to. He will call me out on my excuses and hunt down the answer for me.

And that's what he did.

He's a father, a physician and an oil painter. His painting time has been climbing his priority list in recent years and it's become an area of his life that he's not willing to sacrifice. He makes time for it. He finds energy for it. He makes it important in his life. And I admire that.

So he told me I had to do the same with my writing. He said that instead of worrying how I was going to market a book or if I should start a blog or a podcast or if I should self publish or go the more traditional route, he said I had to just write it. Just write the book. Just do it. Find the time, a little every day. Of course I wasn't going to be able to sneak away for a day here and a day there. I wouldn't be able to knock this thing out over a weekend getaway in the mountains. My children weren't going to give me 3 afternoons a week to write. No. I had to fit it in where I could. That meant knocking out a few hundred words after bedtime every single night and typing out a few paragraphs while the kids ate their toast in the morning.

I just had to write the book and tackle everything else when the book was done.

So that's what I did. And guess what? It actually worked. I let go of all of the stories I had made up about how motherhood was taking up all of my time and energy. I released the thought that I needed to have 3–4 hours of silence to be able to write. Instead, I just wrote here and I wrote there. I knocked out some words during naps and edited whenever I found a few minutes. It wasn't how I thought I would write this book, but it was how I was able to write this book.

 TREADING WATER, HOLDING WEIGHTS

See, I'm still here. The writer in me is still here and it always has been. But it was so easy for so long to let my role as a mother become the reason I couldn't write anymore. It took my husband blatantly calling out my bullshit for me to really understand how I could be a mother, a writer and so much more.

What part of yourself have you been neglecting or placing on hold? Are you making up the same stories that I was? Have you begun to tell yourself that motherhood is worthy of all of your time, all of your energy and all of your passion, and everything else will have to wait until...well... some other day somewhere in the far off future?

It's time to uncover the rest of your layers, maybe even find a few new ones. But remember, you're still there. Motherhood is a part of you, but it's not all of you.

CHAPTER EIGHT

Sex, Ugh: Yeah, it can be hard to fit this in. But make it a priority.

I say "ugh" not because there is anything wrong with sex. No. I say "ugh" because it can be really hard, sometimes nearly impossible, to figure out how to fit sex, and all of intimacy really, into life as a mother. And not finding time and space for intimacy with your partner can cause stress in a relationship. Lots of stress.

Now, if you have a handful of little kids and still maintain a hot and steamy love life, I want to know your secret. If this part of the relationship comes easily to you and you're thinking "Melissa, I have no clue what you're talking about here", then please get a hold of me immediately and let me know what you're doing.

Let me be really clear on this topic: I think sex is great and sex is important. I, however, do not claim to be an expert here, nor do I claim to have this part of my life mastered. It can be a logistical, emotional, energetic, physical and even psychological challenge to figure out exactly how intimacy fits into life as a mother, particularly when your children are all young, sleep is minimal and stress is high. But I believe that this is definitely a part of life that we should dedicate energy to.

So if you've mastered this, or if you're my brother, you can skip this chapter and move on to the next. Just kidding! I don't care who you are or how steamy your relationship is, you can't skip through the good stuff. Keep reading.

My first child was a co-sleeper until the age of five. We threw all of the advice about having kids sleep in their own bed out the window and welcomed him in our bed with us. My husband was knee deep in his medical residency and I was working full-time at a demanding job. Sometimes our nighttime snuggles were the most quality time we got to spend together. But it made intimacy really tough. I was breastfeeding on demand, which was so tiring, and my son liked to wake up all night at all hours to comfort nurse. I was too exhausted to figure out a way out of my exhaustion, so I barely slept.

I remember the advice I'd get:

"It's important for your relationship to get him out of your bed."

"You will sleep much better when he's out of your bed."

"He will sleep much better when he's out of your bed."

"He doesn't need to be nursing at night anymore."

The list went on. It always does, right? Mothers get so much advice, much of it completely unsolicited.

And it was true, we were having a hard time finding time to be intimate. I'm not just talking about sex here, I'm talking about cuddling, holding hands, even just talking.

And it was true, I probably would have slept better with my son in his own bed, maybe. I found myself waking up quite a bit to make sure he was breathing. Moms do that a lot, am I right? I can't even begin to guess the thousands of times I have snuck in to check on my sleeping children, watching their little chests rise and fall, putting my hand up to their mouths to feel that warm exhale, even jabbing my finger at their ribs to feel that heartbeat. I've done it since day one and I'm still doing it. This is what we do.

And it was true, there came a point when he didn't need to nurse at night anymore. But it was a thing we did. So it was just fine.

Regardless, there were as many reasons why this WAS working for us as there were reasons why this WASN'T working for us. And it was a decision we made, so it was the right decision. I believe that's how decisions go, especially in motherhood.

But having sex wasn't always easy. We had to move our kid (sometimes kids). We had to be quiet. We had to tiptoe around in our own bedroom, and no one should have to do that. There was one time I remember our little co-sleeper waking up when we were in the middle of things and I had to roll over and nurse him back to sleep. Then my husband was like 'Hey, are you done over there? Get back over here," and my son wasn't done and he was like "Waaaaahhhhhh!" And my husband was like "How long does this take?" And my son was like "Waaaaahhhhhh!". I was lying in the middle of my husband and my son, both of them needing my attention, but in very different ways and it was all very confusing to me. I just wanted to cry. There is never enough of the mom to go around.

It can be hard to slip into mom mode and then slip into intimate wife mode at the drop of a hat and then flip back again and then back again. Actually, I didn't just find it hard, I found it uncomfortable and psychologically exhausting.

Aside from being needed late at night by both of the guys in my life, I was exhausted from all of life in general. And I felt touched out. I felt like my body was constantly in demand in one way or another, and I just couldn't keep up with it. I wanted all hands off of me, I wanted my boobs back and I wanted to be alone in a dark room where I could just sit and stare at the wall for a few hours of peace. It sounded glorious (and still does).

Was that too much to ask?

But I felt like I was failing everyone, even though I was trying so hard not to. I've heard this same thing from so many other moms. It's amazing that we try in every way to please everyone, to help everyone, to care for everyone. We stretch ourselves thin, and do all we can, and somehow in the end we still feel like we're coming up short. We feel like we are failing everyone.

Sex wasn't top of mind for me. But my husband is wired differently (are they all?) and it was top of mind for him. And it's an important part of a marriage. But this was new territory for us and we didn't know how to navigate it.

Sometimes when you enter new territory, it's easy to get caught up in your own experience of it and forget to consider what it's like for the others involved. And that's where we both found ourselves.

I was completely worn out and couldn't even begin to figure out how to piece myself back together so I could be a good version of myself again.

And my husband was exhausted too, but needed intimacy with me to feel connected and grounded in our relationship.

It took us a long time to figure out what we were dealing with. Instead, I thought he was unreasonable and didn't understand me. He thought I was distant and cold. Ouch! The truth is, parenting is a lot of hard work and it can mess with even the strongest relationships.

   Treading Water, Holding Weights

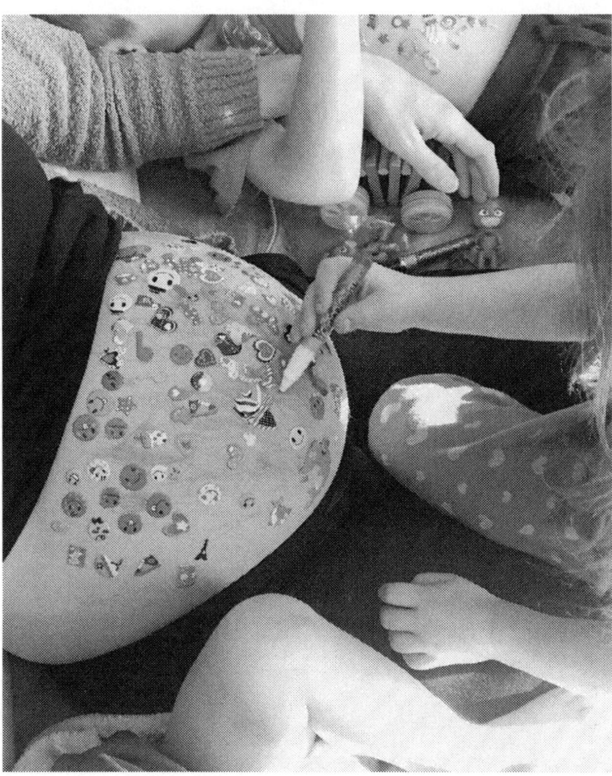

Sometimes we get a little desperate for activities that all three of them enjoy. Luckily my cousin got the kids tattoo pens that kind of wash off (after some legit scrubbing) and someone else got them a million stickers and my belly makes a fabulous canvas right now. So we had a little art time.

Karoh recently turned two and his aunt and gramma sent him a riding tractor. Yesterday Anton and I started assembling it. There is only one way to assemble a riding tractor with your spouse at the end of a long day with three young kids running around, and that one way is to bicker your way through it.

The kids were trying to ride the tractor before we got the pieces out of the box. Karoh was completely happy with just the steering wheel and some loose wheels, and he didn't want to give them up when the directions called for them. Miela stuck skinny markers down the holes of the unassembled tractor, releasing them into the abyss, forever to be heard clunking around in the tractor. Toren enjoyed dumping out all of the small pieces and accidentally, mindlessly scattering them around.

The toolbox was out, which is never ever a safe thing in our house. Not a single one of us belongs near a tool, let alone an entire box of them. Anton and I argued because you cannot possibly stay civil under this kind of pressure.

Then Karoh disappeared into our bedroom, removed his diaper and pooped all over our bed. He peed too, but that's hardly even worth mentioning here. At this point, everyone pees everywhere in my house and I've lowered my standards. But poop. All over my bed. My standards have not yet hit that low. Not yet at least.

Luckily Anton found the disaster scene and, since we were bickering, I pretended to be quite busy with the tractor assembly when he screamed. Usually clean ups of this caliber would be a job for me because I am quite specific and very thorough, but the pressure of the tractor assembly got the best of me and I happily let Anton handle that crisis. I am passive aggressive.

And sometimes you have to pick the lesser of two evils, and last night, the lesser was tractor assembly duty. It is assembled, the kids are thrilled and Anton and I are back on the same team.

. . . .

Can any of you out there relate? Have any of you jumped into motherhood and found that the love and respect you have for your significant other has grown immensely, but the ability to show it in any form has dwindled?

And as we continue to grow as adults, it becomes easier and easier to grow apart if we aren't finding the time to grow together.

Now, I believe that independence is important in relationships. Remember what I wrote in the first few paragraphs of this book about my husband taking an art class once a week that is hilariously called "The 7 Key Folds of Drapery". He is a passionate and talented oil painter. I am not. He loves paging through his many art books on Rembrandt, Caravaggio and Titian. I do not. He pulls up paintings by the masters on the internet and zooms in really close to evaluate the technique. I do not. He takes a

 TREADING WATER, HOLDING WEIGHTS

three hour art class every Thursday night after a full day of work when he's probably quite exhausted and would love to just relax at home. I have never done that and I never will.

. . . .

INSTAGRAM POST JANUARY 27, 2019

If you drive by our house on a Saturday morning, there's a chance you'll see Anton shooing us out the door, throwing snacks and diapers and wipes and extra clothes at us, tossing a stroller in the car, strapping babies in, giving us hurried kisses goodbye before he scurries back into the house, slams the door behind him and locks it.

He will perhaps be wearing his old bathrobe, tattered slippers and hair that points out in every direction. When he is safely inside, he may or may not light incense, blast reggae music and brew some earl grey.

I run around town with the kids for about four hours while he pulls out his oil paints, a canvas and his brushes. He changes the lightbulbs in our home for his painting sessions because he needs the light to be just right for painting. He ignores the dirty breakfast dishes and jumps right in. He's been holding his breath for this moment.

Here is his latest and his absolute greatest. It's 6 feet tall. Where will we hang this? We will find a spot. I posted a picture of him last summer prepping the canvas. Here is the final. A photo doesn't do it justice. He is the strangest, most talented and hilarious man I've ever met.

. . . .

He is growing in his own endeavors separately from me. But we've also made an effort to grow together. I believe that balance is so important in relationships.

And then there's sex. How does sex fit into all of this? Well, obviously it's different for every couple, and I believe it's dependent on so many factors. But instead of making sex this subject that we never talk about together, my husband and I try to address the topic head on. I suggest you do the same. Intimacy can be a tough thing to navigate if we aren't open about our needs, our wants, our concerns, our fears and everything else. It's a little disarming to talk about openly at first, but it makes a difference.

So what can we do? Well, we tried a few things, and sometimes you have to try something out and then change your approach down the road if it's no longer working for you.

We started scheduling our sex. That's what we did. I know it may sound kind of boring and way too predictable, but, well, if we didn't schedule it, it just didn't happen. We decided together on a number of times a week and we picked a few days, and those were the days when we had sex. This wasn't a forever plan for us, but it's what we needed to do at the time. Our children weren't sleeping and we were exhausted and there was nothing left at the end of the day. Our intimacy was taking a hit and we needed to get it back on track.

Guess what? It totally worked. My husband was thrilled because he had certainty around this part of his life. He didn't need to worry about making a move and having me respond with the ever-popular "Not tonight. I'm too tired." We also decided on a number of times per week that made him happy (and probably resulted in the surprise of baby #4). And I

                    TREADING WATER, HOLDING WEIGHTS

really appreciated knowing which nights we were going to be intimate and which nights I could hit the pillow early. On the days we were scheduled, I probably made sure to have an extra cup of coffee in the afternoons and shave my legs. Hey, when you're a mom chasing around children all day, it takes a little planning to feel sexy at night. I can't just switch from snot wiper and diaper changer to hot wife in a moment's notice.

That's what worked for us. We tried other things too. And when one thing wasn't working anymore, we changed it up. I'm sure we'll find ourselves at a point in the future where we have to change it up again. That's fine. Maybe we'll even get back to spontaneity down the road! The point is that we were open and honest about making each other a priority and we were willing to find a solution to this very common problem.

I know it's a common problem. I know of so many other moms struggling with this in their relationships. Some couples just throw in the towel on intimacy and instead become good friends. Some couples bury the problem and slowly come to resent each other. And there are probably many other ways people are dealing with the challenge of maintaining intimacy while being the parents to young children. Whatever you're doing, don't beat yourself up about it if it's not working. This is tough stuff.

Just promise me one thing: if what you're doing right now isn't working for you, you'll start looking for solutions. Intimacy is important. Don't ignore it.

CHAPTER NINE

That Isolation Thing: It's real and raw. Find your way out of it.

Oh, isolation and loneliness is such a tough one in motherhood, particularly when you're new to this mom thing. Remember back to your pre-mom days? Remember having the freedom to stay out late at night with your friends, sleep in on the weekends and take a leisurely brunch around 10am followed by a yoga class and maybe a movie? (Or whatever your version of a fabulous Saturday was!) Those were the days when you could swing by your friend's house at the drop of a hat just to say hi, but had the flexibility to stay as long as you wanted. You were allowed to give all of your attention to conversations. You were well-slept, thinking clearly and uninterrupted. Connection was easy for many of us back then.

But when we become mothers, this whole landscape changes. At least it did for me and many of the mothers I know.

When I had my first child, I didn't have many friends with kids. Actually, I had zero. Motherhood is a massive life change and I struggled to find someone who could relate with the things I was going through. While my friends were doing the usual, my schedule and demands had completely shifted. I was in bed early so I could get up two hours later (and every two hours after that) to nurse my baby. I woke up at 6am because that's when my baby woke up. I juggled diaper changes with breastfeeding with a nap schedule with all of the exhaustion I was feeling. It was a wild time, and I didn't have many people with whom I could talk to about it.

But even when I had my second and third children, and I had other friends who were in the same situation, I still found isolation creeping up on me at times. Sometimes I'm too tired to get out of the house, let alone carry on an adult conversation with anyone, so we hang out at home. Sometimes I find myself at friends' houses, but I'm so preoccupied with my kids that I never really get a chance to have a decent interaction with anyone.

. . . .

INSTAGRAM POST JUNE 28, 2018

I woke up like this. I did. This is me at 6am.

Miela has a horrible cough that kept her up all night...so that kept me up all night... and also Karoh because the three of us slept in this twin bed together. That's right. It was a night of coughing and soothing and nursing and shushing and teething and snuggling and fussing and waking up and waking up and waking up.

 TREADING WATER, HOLDING WEIGHTS

Karoh is on a serious teething mission. He spends his entire day devising plans to eat my hands and chin. That's right, my baby just wants to chew on my CHIN all day long. It's embarrassing to go out in public.

And then Toren joined the party around 6am like a firecracker in a mason jar...a shattered and very fragile mason jar. Despite being the only one in the group who actually slept, he demanded the best snuggle spot and proceeded to kick everyone else, including the mama, which happens to be me the last time I checked.

Ask very little of me today, world. Ask very little.

. . . .

Sometimes it's possible to be so not alone and so entirely alone at the same time.

I don't know about you, but I moved across the country from my entire family. My parents, siblings and nearly all of my extended family are in the Midwest. My husband and I moved to California 10 years ago and we're still here. We do love it here, but we do miss our family dearly.

I envy the other mothers I know who have family just down the street, or even a couple of hours away. But when I've talked to them about isolation and loneliness, they all tell me that they feel it too. So I believe this may be universal in motherhood. It's not necessarily a matter of who lives by you or how close your family is. It's much more about how drastically our schedules and demands change when we become mothers, how our energy and attention is suddenly given so heavily to these little beings we brought into this world.

Often times the feelings of isolation that we experience in motherhood creep up on us. They sneak in unexpectedly and we barely notice them until we are suddenly overwhelmed with loneliness.

Sometimes it's possible to be so not alone and so entirely alone at the same time.

When we become mothers, we agree to take on a massive responsibility. We become responsible for this little human, this tiny baby. Everything else takes a backseat, including our freedom to some extent. The first few weeks and months of motherhood are consumed with figuring out this new role. It's a tremendous addition to our busy lives, one we are eager to make room for. But it's also one that can easily consume our entire days (and nights!), leaving little left for anything else.

As a new mother, I struggled to get enough sleep (still do). There were days when the thought of getting out of the house was so overwhelming for me. I couldn't quite manage to find a window of time between naps, feedings and diaper changes. When I did try to get out of the house, everything took so much longer than I expected.

I didn't have friends who could relate to what I was going through. I tried to meet new mom friends, but it wasn't easy. There was a breastfeeding support group at the hospital that I used to attend every single week. I produced enough milk to feed a football team of babies, so I didn't need support as far as breastfeeding went. But I was so desperate to be around other mothers in an environment where no one was judging me that I went religiously.

My husband was amazingly supportive, but he worked long days and I thought my struggle with feeling isolated was a sign that I was just being a wimp. I couldn't understand what I had to complain about. I had four months of maternity leave away from work where I could essentially do whatever I wanted, as long as I took care of our child.

But none of it was as easy as it sounds. I felt alone and isolated.

So what can we do about this? How can we as mothers find connection and support in motherhood? It's not always easy, but it doesn't have to be hard. The world is connected by this amazing thing called social media. There are groups all over social media, ones specific to where you live, filled with other mamas in your exact same place. The internet gives us amazing tools like meetup.com and other sites where we can join a tribe of mamas like ourselves. There are great local groups, like Stroller Strides, where moms are getting together in person to connect. Sometimes it feels intimidating to take the first step to join one of these groups, but, believe me, you'll be glad you did.

And when we find ourselves at libraries or parks or coffee shops, and we see another mom whom we can relate to, we cannot be afraid to say hi and introduce ourselves. If this feels uncomfortable for you, I definitely encourage you to give it a try. Amazing things can happen when we step outside of our comfort zone.

CHAPTER TEN

Mom Guilt: It comes from every direction. Fight back.

I've lead some retreats for moms in the past. We did a little yoga, some meditation, sound healing, connection with other moms, delicious food and had a chance to dive a bit deeper into this whole motherhood experience. To be honest, running these retreats was one of my favorite things to do for many reasons. The main reason was that in leading these experiences with other moms, I got the chance to sit with mamas and really hear about their version of motherhood. The discussions got deep and really raw.

We talked about what we struggled with in motherhood, what we rocked in motherhood and what we feared. Women came to the retreats from a variety of backgrounds with so many different experiences and lifestyles. But, despite all of the differences, there were so many shared feelings and fears and insecurities among us all as mothers.

Today I had the absolute joy of co-leading our Seed & Song Mom's Mini Retreat with my partner in crime, Laura Anderson. This is the work that keeps me going. This is the work I truly love. It reminds me that we are not alone in our motherhood journeys. We do not need to pretend that every moment is easy, and we do not need to carry the weight of this on our shoulders alone. There is beauty and strength in vulnerability. There is a deep release that happens when we allow ourselves to let go, just a bit, and then a bit more. This is when we become whole again. Thank you mamas. Thank you for this tribe today.

. . . .

These days were emotional, proving to me over and over again that mothers are in a tough spot. The pressures we all feel, the standards we hold ourselves to and what we feel is at stake if we fail, it's a lot. And somehow moms aren't set up to succeed. Sometimes, it feels like we're lugging tremendous weights around on our shoulders, and the odds will be always against us.

But the connection I felt with these moms during our retreats gave me hope. Coming together to grow in motherhood was clearly a step in the right direction.

As I am writing this book, I keep coming back to the question of "What do moms need?" How can I help them? What is it that I can do to have a greater impact on the struggles we are each dealing with individually?

Amazingly, writing this book has given me a chance to dig deep into this question. I've sifted through my own motherhood stories from the past 7 years, relived some of the wildness (which is still very much going on) and asked myself what is it that I need as a mother.

I even polled a number of my mom friends. I asked around to find out what other moms were struggling with. What were their insecurities and challenges in motherhood? The answers were spot on with what I have heard in the past at retreats and what I've experienced in my own walk through motherhood. Here are some that kept popping up:

1. How do I stay centered and calm when my children are acting insane and out of control?
2. How can I be a present mother when life is so busy and I am being pulled in every direction?
3. How can I be involved in my kids' lives and spend quality time with them?
4. Am I a good enough mom?
5. I feel like I'm missing so much and time is flying by. How can I slow it down?
6. How can I have more patience with my kids?
7. How can I stop comparing my child to other kids and myself to other mothers? It steals a lot of joy from situations.
8. How do I balance time with being a mom and working?

Whew! Oh man. That's a lot to take in. Right? I mean, are we enough? Are we loved? Are we loving enough? Can we find more hours in the day? We are already doing all we can, can we do even more? Are we failing our children? Are we horrible at this?

Ugh. I'm exhausted just typing that out.

But I've felt all of these, and more.

ARCHIVED BLOG POST MAY 21, 2017

A woman told me a story. It was about a mother who was having a tough day, like we all do. She yelled a bit more than she wanted to. There were more time-outs and fewer snuggles, more frustration and fewer smiles. You know those days. They're the ones filled with stress and tension and exasperation. At the end of those days, we collapse onto our beds and wonder what we could have done differently. We feel sad, perhaps confused, maybe a little guilty. And on that day, that mother's son turned to her and asked, 'Do you even like being a mom?' He asked it matter-of-factly. He was serious. He wanted to know.

Oh man. Of course she does. Of course. Right? It's just that in that moment, on that day, it wasn't easy. It was so very hard and sometimes it feels like too much to handle. If we stop and think about it, we know it will pass and the good moments are around the corner. But our little ones can't always see that. They can't always understand that life comes with ups and life comes with downs, and motherhood is no different. The dark moments make the bright ones shine even brighter. But we have to realize that sometimes our darkness feels too dark for them. There are so many lessons we can teach our children on these tough days. There's so much they can learn about life, about love and emotions.

But it means we must take a breath, then another. We must pull ourselves out of the fury and let the anger dissolve a bit. It's through example that we help our children learn to navigate the ups and downs of life. When we are honest about our emotions and our struggles, we help them to understand that there are ways to move through the darkness toward the light. It's hard. We get wrapped up in the darkness and sometimes it feels like that's all that there is.

That's not all there is.

So soften just a bit and talk about the challenging moments. Tell them when things aren't easy. Let them know. They're perceptive. They probably already know, but let them hear it from you. And then find a way to move through that darkness together.

They will surprise you.

 TREADING WATER, HOLDING WEIGHTS

Here's a picture from a darker day when I thought my children were literally going to break my back.

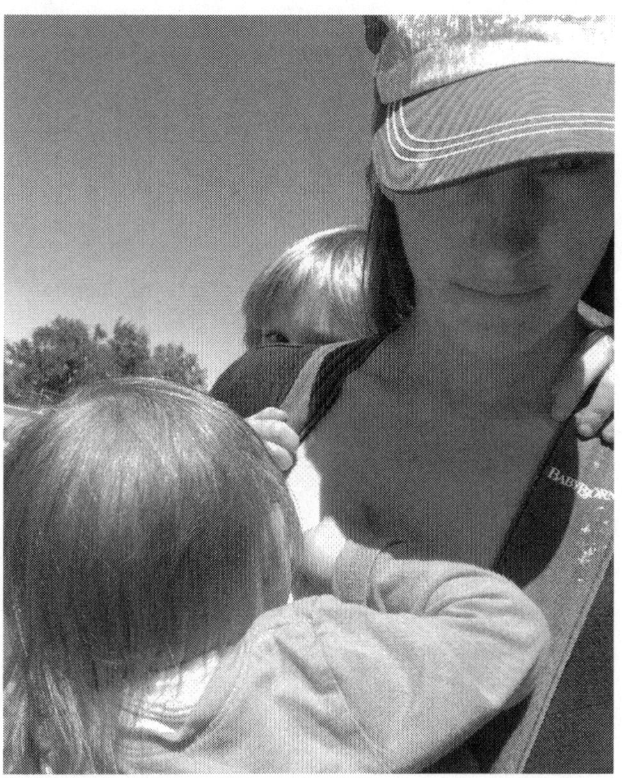

I went to the library today trying to find a book that would help me understand how to survive motherhood. I needed something that would help me with ME, not something that would help me with my children. The book I was looking for had to speak to motherhood specifically, it needed to be on the same page as me here. I wanted something that could relate to what I was going through, help me to understand mom guilt and the constant second-guessing of every decision I made. It needed to call out the bullshit in motherhood and equip me with what I needed to stay sane and at peace in the midst of this all.

So I started in the Parenting section, which was right between the Cooking section and the Business section. Being a parent, it seemed like a logical first step. I found books like *Raising Resilient Children, How to be a Great Parent, How to Raise Successful People, Raising Can-Do Kids* and even a book called *The Power of Presence*, which I thought might have some tips, until I read the subtitle: *Be a Voice in Your Child's Ear Even When You're Not with Them.* No, no, no. I was looking for books about parenting as it related to ME. I didn't need something that taught me how to raise top-notch kids. I needed something that taught me how to not lose my absolute shit every time my toddler threw a tantrum at Target while my three year old climbed on mannequins and my six year old asked me to play Yahtzee with him for the 10 millionth time. I needed something very specific to THAT scenario.

More books about nursing, raising happy babies, managing sleep schedules (possibly something I should look at), potty training, newborns, toddler tantrums and raising independent kids. Ok, ok, so all of these most likely have useful tidbits in them. But what I needed was something that spoke to me and about me as a parent.

The next book looked spot on. This was it! The title was *Hiding in the Bathroom.* 'Yes' I thought, 'that's me! That's my life. This book gets me.' But upon further inspection, I realized it was a book about introverts. I was beginning to get into the Business section. That Parenting section proved to be a bust.

Ok, where else to look? Let's see. Guilt, anxiety, patience, fear, overall mental (in)stability. We're getting into psychology here. Off to visit that section, right between Computer Science and Religion. I found a book called *Guilt, Shame and Anxiety.* We're getting closer. Now can we just add "In Motherhood" at the end of that and possibly include something in there to lighten the mood?

Next book: *So You've Been Publicly Shamed.* Yes, yes, this is me. This is getting closer. I have been publicly shamed by my children so many times. This wasn't the book though.

Then on to *Mothers: An Essay on Love and Cruelty.* I was thrilled to see that it spoke to mothers and also the highs and lows. But when I opened it up, it was a bit of a snoozer and missed the mark. I needed some self-help mixed in there, maybe some humor to keep me interested.

Off to *Rage Becomes Her.* Kind of exactly what I was feeling this morning while I was getting the kids ready for school. I don't need to elaborate on this rage at all. You mothers know exactly what I'm talking about. The rage is real. But this book was about the power of women's anger. I needed something to help me chill the heck out, not convince me of my rage-filled power. I didn't even open the cover. Next.

On to *Inner Peace for Busy Women: Balancing Work, Family and your Inner Life*. But the author decided to publish every single word in the color GREEN and I just can't ask myself to read that. But before closing the book, I did glance at the line "The more stress women feel, short of disorienting hysteria, the more we bond,"[*] and I can relate to that. This morning on the walk home from dropping my oldest off at school, I was with my good friend, and I just off-loaded everything on her about this morning with my crazy kids. I used so many f-bombs and it was all very animated. It wasn't "disorienting hysteria", but it was kind of close. When we got to the corner of our streets, where we parted ways, I was like 'Wow, thank you for letting me vent. I feel so much better.' She smiled sweetly back at me, the kind of real smile that you don't actually get from people that often, and said 'Oh, that was venting?' And she went on her way. That's bonding.

After that, I went to the coffee shop to continue writing this book, and I realized that if no one else had written the book I was looking for at the library, then I had to. And then I realized that I already was writing it. I mean, this book is about shifting our perspective on motherhood so that we can move away from the stuff we struggle with and towards the stuff we want more of. It's about kicking mom guilt to the curb, letting go of our insecurities, being ok with some chaos, accepting that we are not perfect and finding ways to open up to the people around us instead of closing down and getting buried by motherhood.

....

[*] Borysenko, Joan Z. *Inner Peace for Busy Women: Balancing Work, Family and your Inner Life.* Carlsbad, CA: Hay House, 2005.

I am having a VERY glamorous version of motherhood this morning.

Miela was up at 4:45 and wanted a fort and a snuggle. I delivered on the fort, but told her I just couldn't crawl in there with her. My pregnant belly is too big and mom needs a few minutes in the morning. But no, she wouldn't have it.

Anton chimed in with 'Oh come on, she won't always want you to climb in forts and snuggle. Just do it.' I informed him that I do this stuff all day long with her, so that reasoning has absolutely zero effect on me.

Regardless, I'm a sucker so I crawled in. Actually, it's more like I heaved myself in. It wasn't easy or graceful and the fort was really hot and far too small for me.

There are some situations where our kids want us to do something and we say 'yes' because they won't always be small and they won't always want us to do this stuff with them. But this is definitely not one of those situations. Don't let mom guilt steal your well-deserved 5 minutes of peace, mamas. You're stronger than that.

So let's talk specifically about combatting mom guilt and telling our motherhood insecurities to piss off.

Where does mom guilt come from?

This question is probably the correct place to start if we're going to put up a fight against mom guilt. Or maybe it's more about RELEASING mom guilt than putting up a fight against it. Regardless, if we want to deal with it, we need to understand where it's coming from. So for this, I turned to an EXPERT. I may have my theories here, but I also know when to reach out to people who have actually been educated and trained in this stuff.

So this is when I divulge one of my secret weapons in life: my sister Emily. She's a part-time farmer and part-time marriage and family therapist, living in Cottage Grove, WI. And she's my go-to for marriage and parenting advice. Sure, I have my friends and my mom and even my other sisters. (Dear other sisters, you are both my secret weapons in other ways, so don't freak out and passive aggressively leave all of appetizer prep to me on our next family vacation. Don't be like that.)

Ok, back to my farmer/therapist sister. Yesterday I asked her about this whole mom guilt thing. I laid out a few theories I had read on insecurities and asked for her input. As usual, she delivered gold. Here's my interpretation of what she had to say about it all:

Insecurities arise in all of us. Start there. Know that we all feel insecure, even those of us who seem the most secure. These insecurities arise when we don't think we're enough or when we don't think we're doing something the way we should be doing it. Anyone out there relate to that in motherhood?

These insecurities arise when we don't think we're enough or when we don't think we're doing something the way we should be doing it.

I swear, this whole "not enough" business is spot on for me. I have done marketing consulting part-time from home and also taught yoga off and on over the past few years in between being a mom and a wife. Even when we got to the point where my income wasn't necessary for us to make ends meet, I kept taking clients and teaching yoga classes and retreats. I think I wanted so desperately to hold on to these parts of my identity. Beyond being a mother and a wife, I wanted to do and be more. I thought it was really important for me, and consulting and teaching yoga felt like the right things to do. And they were, in many ways, a great way to add more layers to my onion. They filled me up and made me feel more complete.

But in some ways, they also made me feel like I wasn't enough. I felt like I was stretched so thin that I wasn't actually doing a good job at any one thing. I felt like I was failing at everything a little bit. I realize this failure and sense of not being enough might have been 100% in my head. If you asked my clients, yoga students and even my family, I don't actually think any of them would say I was failing them. But it always felt to me like I was never able to give what I wanted to give to any one area of my life. Sound familiar?

And that's a hard place to be, particularly when your children and husband are some of the people you feel like you're letting down. These insecurities can be pretty brutal, but they're something that we all face from time to time.

I felt like I was stretched so thin that I wasn't actually doing a good job at any one thing.

I am hiding from my children. This has been...a...day. I sent Anton a photo of us in the midst of total chaos this morning. He replied that I looked traumatized. I was. I am.

At school drop off, another mom told me I looked really pale and asked if I was ok. I told her that I was fine, but that my kids spent the morning falling apart repeatedly. (They then went on to do that all day.) I asked her why all of the other moms seemed to have things under control. She reminded me that none of them really do. And then I remembered that we're all just different versions of disasters on any given day. Somehow it makes me feel better knowing that this kind of chaos has company.

So if today was...a...day for you too, you're not alone and, also, chances are that things will look better for us tomorrow. We might be one of those mamas at the grocery store with a cart full of happy, peaceful children smiling up at us while we laugh back at them, tossing our washed, properly dried AND brushed hair over our shoulders and handing them a gallon of organic, grass-fed milk in a glass container to carefully put in the cart, while another mom angrily pushes her squeaky cart past us, screaming at her kids to 'get back here!' with horrible bed-head, wearing saggy sweatpants and loading up on the cheapest, easiest microwave meals available. But don't judge, that'll be us next week.

Smile on the good days, and hide in your sweatshirt on the rough days.

(My children are eating dried pasta and watching Netflix right now. Don't try to tell me you've never been there. What? You haven't? Oh, yeah, no, I was just kidding. We'd never do that? Dried pasta?! Netflix?! No. No. Yeah, no. I wasn't serious.)

And you can't comment something like 'Hang in there mama!' For crying out loud, of course I'm going to do that. Instead tell me the most outrageous, maddening thing your child did this week. That's what I want to hear. Because, remember, this kind of chaos likes company.

. . . .

So what do we do about it? Well, back to what the farmer/therapist said:

My sister said that insecurities are the parts of ourselves that we don't like, and we work really hard to keep these parts hidden from others. We don't think our true self is enough to be loved, so we start to create a false self to hide the pieces we are insecure about and ashamed of.

Whew! We do all that?

Yes. We do.

I'm sure that we all have shadows. I know I do. Shadows are the darker parts of ourselves, maybe the parts we're embarrassed of or the parts we don't like. And somehow, we've convinced ourselves that we absolutely CANNOT let others see these shadows or the world will end.

Ok, farmer/therapist, so we are afraid of not being enough and not being loved. We pinpoint the parts of ourselves we don't like and pretend they don't exist. Then we build up this fake version of ourselves as protection. But this isn't us and this doesn't feel right. So what do we do?

It's time to call out our insecurities so we can embrace them as a part of ourselves. That's right. If we can accept these shadows and be compassionate with ourselves, we can then decide if we want to keep them as they are, or change them. But first, we have to go easy on ourselves and start with a little self-love.

     TREADING WATER, HOLDING WEIGHTS

Do you follow? Let's look at an example. Say your greatest insecurity in motherhood is not spending enough time with your kids. In fact, this one has come up frequently with the mothers I've spoken to about insecurities in motherhood. Maybe you work full-time and need to do that in order to help provide for your family. You go in to work around 8am and don't finish until 6pm. The guilt piles up and you constantly beat yourself up inside about not being there enough for your kids.

Here's a little exercise to walk yourself through:

> **Step 1:** Acknowledge it and embrace it. Say to yourself "Yeah, I'm not getting enough time with my kids. It is what it is and I cannot do everything as perfectly as I'd like to. That's reality for us right now."
>
> Sometimes Step 1 can be a tough one because it feels like we're giving ourselves permission to do the things we don't like about ourselves. But the truth is, when we're motivated to do something by being really hard on ourselves, we may be able to create short-term changes, but we won't be able to cultivate long-term changes. If we want long-term changes, we have to come from a place of compassion.
>
> So instead of yelling at yourself about being away from your children, find your peace with it. Don't try to change it yet. First, open up your arms and welcome it in as a part of your life.
>
> **Step 2:** Decide what you're going to do about it. Sometimes, you may decide to make changes. Sometimes, you may decide that you are not going to make changes. But whatever you decide, you're making that decision from a place of compassion instead of a place of guilt and resentment.

So if you're that mom working full-time who feels really guilty about not spending enough time with her children, accept this as a part of yourself. Give yourself a chance to take a deep breath and shed any guilt you feel about it. Then you decide what you're going to do about it. Maybe you decide to change something about your work schedule. Or perhaps that isn't the route you go and you decide to make extra efforts to really bond and be present during nights and weekends. Or maybe you find another solution that works for your family.

Or you may decide that no changes can be made and you're going to continue on with everything as it is. Whatever you choose, you are coming from a place of compassion with yourself instead of a place of not being good enough.

And that, mama, is a much better feeling. The mom guilt slowly starts to melt away and conscious, compassionate acceptance emerges. This is a much better thing to carry around on your shoulders than guilt.

We are able to have compassion towards our children when they come to us with their insecurities. We look them in the eyes, hold them and speak sweetly, asking what is going on. We listen carefully, let them know they are loved and there is nothing to worry about. Then we help them decide how to move forward.

I mean, if we do it for them, why can't we do it for ourselves? Why can't we speak to ourselves like we're a five year old who still wets the bed and feels ashamed. Try it out.

That was a lot about mom guilt and insecurities. I could go on. My farmer/therapist sister could go on. Maybe one day we will, but for now, I leave you with these parting words on this subject: Just like with sex, if something isn't working for you, change it. As mothers, we carry so much on our shoulders. There's no extra room for things like guilt and insecurities. It's time to dust those shoulders off and lighten our load a bit.

Whatever you choose, you are coming from a place of compassion with yourself instead of a place of not being good enough.

CHAPTER ELEVEN

Oh, Some Stillness: You should find this or you will explode.

When I was little, my mother said to me constantly, "Think before you speak." I never did, no matter how many times she told me this. I said the first thing that came into my mind, and the thought of doing anything else didn't make any sense to me. I was emotional and dramatic and never held anything in. Now, this isn't exactly a bad thing. Sometimes those tendencies come in handy in life. I was never afraid to say how I felt. I was pretty open and honest. I certainly didn't bottle up my negative emotions, that's for sure. Instead I just sprayed them all over those who were around me. But as I grew older, I found that my inability to process anything in my brain before I put it out into the world could get me into situations I wasn't exactly thrilled about.

My emotions felt out of control at times. They ruled me. I felt them very intensely and wasn't sure how to process them. If I was angry, everyone knew it. If I didn't like someone, I didn't exactly hide it. I lacked tact and had a very blunt approach to life, taking on a "well, this is how I am, try to deal with it" attitude to everything. And then one day I was like 'Oh, I'm not sure I like myself that much.' I mean, I liked parts of me, but there were some parts I really wasn't too fond of. It finally dawned on me that I could probably change those parts with a little effort. Just because I had associated with one pattern for many years of my life, didn't mean I couldn't let that pattern go and move on to something that felt more congruent with the life I wanted to live.

Life handed me a great opportunity to make this shift in life. One winter, I was involved in a horrible head-on car accident with a semi-truck on the highway while I was moving to Minneapolis, Minnesota. I received a prescription for Vicodin and was told to go to physical therapy. My doctor informed me that I may have to live with my pain for the rest of my life. I was 23 years old. I couldn't grocery shop because standing up for more than 30 minutes was excruciating. One day I tried to go shopping at the Mall of America and was overwhelmed with the amount of ground to cover and the pain I was feeling. I had been an athlete my entire life, all through college, and this felt pretty devastating.

My Vicodin prescription was never filled. I couldn't bring myself to do that. I found physical therapy very frustrating and minimally helpful. Someone suggested I give yoga a try. At this point, I was up for anything that might be useful. I walked in to my first yoga class at the Yoga Center of Minneapolis and walked out feeling amazing.

I remember the teacher gently guiding me through seated twists. She asked me to find length on my inhale and twist on the exhale. Then she helped me to open my hamstrings like I've never experienced before. Moving with the breath and finding the softness to ease my way through the tension was such a new and novel idea.

I had always been a serious athlete. But, I often chatted my way through stretches before and after soccer games. I mindlessly reached for my toes after a long run. I might give my quadriceps a nod with a quick stretch and maybe even help my calves release a little tension, too. But this was all done without much thought.

I had never really connected with my body and my breath in the way this yoga teacher was asking me to. I couldn't believe it, but the horrible heaviness I had been feeling in my back felt lighter. It wasn't gone, but this was the one thing that had given me actual relief since that semi-truck took me down like a bowling pin.

I was hooked on it after that. I returned to the studio the next day, and immediately decided to enroll in yoga teacher training, not because I wanted to teach yoga, but because yoga felt like the thing that might heal my body, and I needed to know everything about it.

The thing I didn't expect was that yoga and meditation would also heal my crazy mind and wild emotions. They would open up doors to me that I didn't know existed in the world and, well, within myself too.

And all of this was so instrumental in my experience of motherhood, because motherhood is full of moments that test you to the core, every last part of you.

. . . .

INSTAGRAM POST JULY 16, 2019

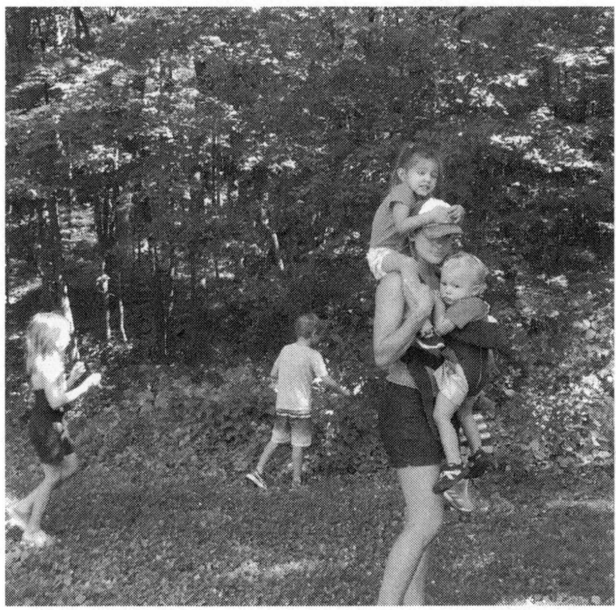

Today we went hiking at Devil's Lake. At the exact moment this picture was taken (and probably the moments before and after this was snapped) I can't see a thing because Miela refuses to come down from my shoulders and will not even consider taking her hands off my eyes. We didn't even make it to the hiking trail and Miela threw herself on the ground screaming, 'I can't walk or run or stand up.' She wanted us to know that anything we might toss her way was 100% out of the question. 'Can you run?' No. 'Well perhaps if you can't run, you can walk?' No. 'Perhaps if you can't walk, you can at least stand up.' No. Definitely not. So she continued to sit on my shoulders and cover my eyes while I did my best to keep going.

I had my first little breakdown of our 4+ week family trip today. All of the kids needed everything at once, and Toren couldn't figure out how to behave for just a moment, and it's very hot, and everyone has mosquito bites, and we're camping, so a solid break down from the mom was in order. I usually fall apart about 3 times on these long, 4 week trips back to Wisconsin each summer, so going this long without anything yet is probably a record for me.

I'm past due for a good fight with my mom, some snarky words exchanged with my sister and a long restorative yoga class where I take a few deep breaths and walk out feeling 150% better.

Wait, you didn't think I survived 4 weeks in Wisconsin with 3 kids solo without some legit meltdowns of my own, did you?! I totally support the occasional adult meltdown. Toddlers can't be the only ones who get to do that.

. . . .

When I was new to yoga and meditation, it was tough for me. I bet this could be said for anyone who is new to mindfulness of any sort, specifically if you're used to a very busy and frantic speed of life. The slow pace, the moments spent in stillness, my busy mind jumping from one thing to the next, all of these things made me feel like I was failing at this whole endeavor. When I got frustrated with the practice, I found myself saying in my head little things like 'This is just a silly fad,' and 'I'm too busy for this,' and 'I should really be making dinner right now,' because I thought those were the things that mattered most. I didn't know any better.

But something kept telling me to stay right where I was and to keep going, and I actually listened to that little voice. I kept going. I returned to that yoga studio and sat through meditations and absorbed as much as I could about this new part of existence.

And the changes in me were pretty drastic. I felt them and people around me did too. I stopped living such an emotionally charged life. I was less reactive and much more thoughtful in my interactions. I developed more empathy and compassion for people, and myself too. I started to feel things, like peace and contentment. I was generally more chilled out, which was pretty sensational for me. I felt like, for the first time in my life,

    TREADING WATER, HOLDING WEIGHTS

I had an idea of who I was and what my operating principles were in life, which made it so much easier to make decisions both big and small.

Now, translate all of this stuff into motherhood. These are all the kinds of things we want to have in our pockets when our toddlers are smearing poop across the bathroom walls and our six year olds are doing parkour in the kitchen while pasta is boiling on the stove and the dishes are carefully balanced, drying in the dish rack.

. . . .

INSTAGRAM POST DECEMBER 26, 2019

I feel like this polar bear gets me right now. It's my spirit animal. I'm not talking about all polar bears, just this exact one.

I have a friend who hosts a podcast about the (mis)adventures of dating and the advice that goes along with it. She's hilarious and witty and the kind of person I want to have over for morning coffee that turns into lunch that turns into pizza for dinner and ends with a couple of bottles of wine and a karaoke bar. She's just hilarious. I find that listening to her podcast is a comical break from the chaos of motherhood and a peek into the chaos of single life. Trading one chaos for the other, that's what we do.

And I needed that trade today. When we travel, the sleeping arrangements turn into a big game of twister and musical chairs. Last night I woke up to a large piece of one of my kids' poop in my bed. Not poop in someone's diaper or smeared on someone's leg. No, this was just a huge turd in my bed. This is not the kind of thing that should ever happen to anyone, ever. Ever.

Right now I'm going to tell you what I did about the poop, and I don't want you to speak to me of this ever again. It stays right here. I picked it up with my hand and walked to the bathroom. My bare hand. I did. Halfway to the bathroom, I stopped, woke up a little more and realized I was carrying a big piece of poop in my bare hand. I hung my head a little as I reflected on the new depths my standards have plunged to.

But this is indeed motherhood and some of you are nodding, thinking 'I've done that' or 'I've done worse' or maybe even just 'yeah, I get it'. And then some of you are horrified and will never look at me the same way. It's ok. I bet you've done worse. Or you will some day. Or your mom probably did, for sure.

. . . .

Most of us moms out there (or possibly ALL of the moms out there) have reacted emotionally and negatively to our children. It's hard not to. And after the fact, we realized that we probably scared the crap out of them a bit.

Mindfulness trains us to be less reactive. It gives us the ability to pause briefly before we respond to the poop and parkour attempts, and in this pause, we get to make a conscious decision about how we want to react. So, instead of screaming "what the eff" at your two year old when they lick the floor at O'Hare airport in Chicago, you can take a breath and say the things you'd really like to say. I'm not sure what exactly you'd like to say when your child licks the floor at O'Hare airport. Is there really anything to say in that moment? Are there words? At least a little mindfulness in your life

  TREADING WATER, HOLDING WEIGHTS

will give you a moment to consider those questions instead of immediately wailing and flailing around uselessly.

And mindfulness helps us with distraction too. This world is full of distractions. Everything from phones to advertisements to the frantic pace of our busy minds, all of these things work constantly to pull us out of the present moment. But presence is really all our kids want from us, and if we stop to think about it, we want to give them all of the presence we can.

Mindfulness doesn't ask us to live fully in every single moment. No. Instead, mindfulness lets us know when we're distracted. It's like a little light that goes on saying 'Hey! You're pretty detached from this actual moment and instead focusing entirely on that thing that happened three days ago,' or 'You're very busy scrolling through the lives of your friends on your phone, but you're missing this moment right here in front of you.' And with that awareness, you get to decide what's next. You may decide to stay distracted, or you may make the decision to snap out of the past, future or your social media feed, and step in to the present moment that you're living in. You get to decide. But without mindfulness, this awareness doesn't kick in as easily and you're coasting through your days, and Instagram, on autopilot.

Beyond the benefits that a mindfulness practice will have on your parenting style, it will also do wonders for you specifically. The research behind mindfulness is quite astounding, really. Some of the benefits of a consistent mindfulness practice include:

- Reduced stress, depression and anxiety
- Increased immune system and brain functioning
- Lowered blood pressure and heart rate
- Enhanced awareness, attention and focus
- Overall experience of connection, peace and stillness

I could basically use all of those things in my life, and I know a lot of other moms out there who would agree. Stress, depression and anxiety are huge challenges that come with motherhood. These can be tough battles to fight, and often times we struggle to find ways to cope with them.

Brains that don't seem to function properly, yeah, sign me up for that one. My mental clarity and overall intelligence has plummeted in recent years.

I'm not sure about my heart rate or blood pressure, but I'd like to be around for as long as possible on this earth, so please help me out there too.

And while I sometimes think that my ability to be aware of everything that's going on around me, give attention to the task at hand and focus on all of the moving pieces in my family is razor sharp, I know that I'm really burnt out and my mind isn't actually managing all of this as exceptionally as I think.

I would most definitely like a little more connection, peace and stillness in my life. There are days, maybe even weeks when those words don't even feel like a part of my vocabulary.

So if mindfulness does all of this, how come we aren't all on this train already? Why weren't we taught this in school and how come it's not a staple in our lives already?

Well, perhaps mindfulness is new to you. Or perhaps you know all of this, but, like me at times, you find it really easy to make up a million reasons why we don't have time for a mindfulness practice. We can't slow down or stop. We have to keep going or the world will crumble? Right? At least that's what we tell ourselves.

Well, dear mama, you should find time for it, both for yourself and for your children. Incorporate it into your life and model it for your kids so they do the same. I swear it's one of the keys to keeping your head above water in motherhood, because sometimes motherhood is just like treading water, holding weights. Let me explain...

Last summer I was vacationing in South Haven, Michigan with my extended family. We have done this every single summer for the past 35 years. A group of about 60 of us take over a little vacation place up on the bluffs overlooking Lake Michigan. We basically sit around all day, eat good food, swim, laugh, sit around all day and sit around all day. It's a glorious week. I'm lucky to have a huge, loud, happy family that loves to come together.

I was in the pool with my youngest, Karoh, who was one year old at the time. We were out in the deep end of the pool floating together on a raft. I decided to swim over to the edge of the pool to talk with one of my cousins. So I swam off of the raft, holding on to Karoh with one arm and paddling with the other. I'm a good swimmer, but I didn't think this through very well. It was hard, really hard.

     Treading Water, Holding Weights

He was having so much fun in the water, and I didn't have very far to go. I thought it would be easier. But suddenly I felt my head starting to go under. I wanted to keep Karoh above water. I couldn't let him go down. And I didn't want to cause a scene. I was fine. Things were fine. I could do this.

But suddenly I wasn't sure I could. Even in the water, Karoh started to feel heavy, and I was doing everything I could to tread water while still hold the weight of him with his head above water AND not cause a scene. Everything was ok. I mean, we were ok, I think.

Finally, after what felt like 25 minutes but was only about 7 seconds, I got us over to the edge of the pool and carried on a conversation with my cousin. In my head, I was like 'Wow, that was a little wild.' And then I realized that this, indeed, was what motherhood felt like for me: treading water, holding weights—half swimming, half treading water, trying to keep my child safe and happy, trying to act as if everything is ok even when things aren't. The weight of it all was pushing me down, but it was a weight I was happy to hold and determined to keep safe.

Now, I'm not trying to compare motherhood to a near drowning experience with my child. Well, maybe I am. But actually, I wasn't going to drown. There were people around me whom I could have asked for help. I was actually quite capable of handling what I was doing, it just felt like a lot in the moment.

But here's how yoga and meditation, actually let's just call it "mindfulness" (because I think that's what I really found through yoga and meditation), plays such an important role in motherhood. Motherhood is all-encompassing at times. Similar to how I felt in that pool, as mothers, we are holding the most important thing in the world, and we are making decisions and choices every single day to keep this beautiful child safe, happy and thriving.

Mindfulness gives us a moment to step outside of that heaviness and find things like clarity, peace, perspective and release.

But motherhood is also really heavy, both in the ways I've already discussed in this book and in so many other ways. Mindfulness gives us a moment to step outside of that heaviness and find things like clarity, peace, perspective and release. In the stillness, we are able to connect with the core of what we are as mothers, and that's something that we can't easily do when we're wiping dirty bottoms, making mac & cheese and nursing teething babies at all hours of the day.

Ok, ok, hold on. I know finding the time to meditate feels impossible. And I realize that sitting in stillness isn't exactly at the top of everyone's to do list. So maybe your version of mindfulness isn't the typical style of mediation. Maybe it's gardening or walking or listening to quiet music while you attack that mound of dirty dishes. Perhaps mindfulness is sitting quietly at night snuggling your toddler while they fall asleep and you take 20 full breaths at the same time. Or if your children are just a little older and perhaps ready for three minutes of meditation, choose from one of the 10 billion free meditation for kids audios out there available as a podcast or on Spotify or whatever, and listen to it with your kids. Maybe it's even a movement practice or involves music or writing in some way.

But whatever your version of mindfulness is, whatever you can do to find a little peace and stillness, do it. Make it a part of your routine and stick with it. There will be moments when you look at the floor that desperately needs to be swept, and it could be so easy for you to choose that floor over your few minutes of mindfulness. But don't do it! Be strong. Stick with your routine.

Find something that gets you a little stillness. Schedule it every day. Then do it. Start today.

Otherwise, I'm telling you, you're going to explode.

INSTAGRAM POST SEPTEMBER 11, 2018

I've only taught a few restorative yoga classes since having Karoh. I love teaching and I miss teaching. But instead of jumping back into teaching yoga, I decided to jump back into being a student. Instead of leading classes, I'm taking classes. Instead of giving, I'm receiving. Instead of pouring out my heart, I'm letting my heart soak it all in. Instead of sharing bits and pieces of my mind and soul, I'm just receiving what others are called to share.

And it's amazing. In tonight's class, the teacher said that we must release all of our energy at times so that we have it available to us when we need it, when we need to call upon it to lift us up and those around us.

Oh. That makes sense. But I don't do that. Instead I flip on my high energy switch the moment I open my eyes in the morning and I don't flip it off until my head hits the pillow at night. And since I'm a mom, I'm up about 6 times each night nursing a baby and assuring a toddler that the imaginary bunny from her dream isn't hungry.

So this thing called restorative yoga, this amazing practice that I believe so whole-heartedly in, we really do need it. All of us do. How can we expect our energy to be there for us when we need it if we aren't releasing it from time to time? We can't run on high all day (and night). We need moments, outside of when we are asleep, when we are letting that energy go, when we are slowing down and asking nothing of ourselves. It sounds so luxurious, but it's not. It's a necessity.

I could go on and on about this, but Miela needs me to feed her obnoxious imaginary bunny. Thank you Woven We Are yoga studio in Carlsbad for yet another great experience.

· ·

Find the things that preserve your sanity in a healthy way, and I am certain some sort of a mindfulness practice is the answer here. The farmer/therapist recently recommended an app to me called Mindfulness Coach. Honestly, I'd love to be able to tell you that I've been using it for 2 months and I love it, but I only downloaded it today so I can't really say much about it. But I'm going to give it a try. If the farmer/therapist recommends it, there's a solid chance it's a good option. She doesn't make recommendations lightly.

Find the things that preserve your sanity in a healthy way . . .

   TREADING WATER, HOLDING WEIGHTS

A little Monday yoga sequence to get me grounded, balanced and tapped into the present moment. Ah, the peace. Thank goodness for a few moments away from the chaos so I can just focus on myself. Five seconds after these pics were taken, a huge pile of sand fell out of Miela's pocket and right into my eyeballs. Namaste.

CHAPTER TWELVE

Advice from All Angles: Do you remember when I asked your advice on motherhood? Me neither.

This chapter was a little bit tricky to write. Do you know why? Because it's taken me a while to figure out how I feel about all of the advice moms get and also how I want to deal with this inundation of advice in my own life. We're bombarded with it. Some days I welcome it with open arms, and some days I'm exhausted by it.

Mothers get advice from other moms and other dads. We get advice from our own parents and our family, both near and far. As moms, we get advice from doctors and nurses, professionals and experts. We get it from friends and non-friends, neighbors and strangers. It comes from the man in the grocery store and the woman at the library. Advice comes from those who have been up all night with newborns themselves and, oddly, from those who have never even held a newborn. We get advice from social media and blogs and newsletters and magazines and books.

Some of this advice comes from people who know us well and some comes from people whom we've never seen before. This advice may have been tested out and proven to work, or it may be a theory that someone came up with that they think has the groundbreaking potential to change the world of child-rearing. The person offering this advice may come from a place of selflessness and love, or they may come from a place of merely enjoying the sound of their own voice, no matter what they're saying. Some advice comes from people who know us as mothers and understand our lives. Some of this advice does not.

. . . not everything works for everyone.

Mothers have been around for quite a while now. We aren't new to this world by any means, and many of the challenges we face have been faced by women before. I am 100% in favor of drawing upon the wisdom of those who have walked this path before, for sure. That wisdom can be like gold. It can change sleepless nights into 6 hour stretches of uninterrupted slumber. It can change fussy, unhappy newborns into sweet little bundles of joy whom we can bring with us to the grocery store and then maybe even on a quick Target run afterwards.

My mother tells me that my great-grandmother used to be able to soothe my colicky sister like no one else. She turned her over on her knee and bounced her up and down repeatedly, and there was no crying. Brilliant, and it probably gave my mom some much needed moments of relief. I tried this with my first born and it worked. He loved it. I tried it with my second born, and she despised it and hasn't looked at me the same way since.

Babies are all different. So, not everything works for everyone.

Sleep deprivation hit me really hard, especially with my first born. I was too wound up when he would nap to take any sort of nap myself, and my anxiety and fear that he would absolutely stop breathing at any moment kept me up all night checking on him. My mom would always tell me "You have to sleep when he sleeps." Maybe that worked for her. Perhaps that's what she did when her children were napping babies. But the thought, at that time, was too hard for me to fathom. When would the dishes get done? Who would do the laundry? When would I eat? Who would check on my sleeping child 35 times to make sure his tiny chest was still rising and falling with each inhale and exhale? It had to be me, so that meant I couldn't catch up on sleep. EVER. My anxiety was the problem. The advice only frustrated me (Mom, it did). Then when I had two children, I tried to take her advice, but the stinkers never slept at the same time, or at least rarely.

  Treading Water, Holding Weights

JOURNAL ENTRY DECEMBER 26, 2017

Nap-trapped

'Sleep when they sleep,' that's what my mom always tells me. When the babies take naps, that's when you're supposed to take one too. And it sounds like a good idea. It really does. I'm a mother of two young children and I'm up a lot with them at night, so this all makes a lot of sense.

But here's the thing, my kids NEVER EVER sleep at the same time. My one year old sleeps a very solid two hours in the afternoon. And my four year old wants nothing to do with sleep and fights naps like his life depends on it. I have spent hours driving him around trying to get him to sleep. I've stared at him in the rear view mirror while I'm slowly cruising down the street, willing his head to nod off. I've watched numerous tv shows with him, snuggled up, watching his little eyelids and praying they'd get heavy enough to stay shut for a solid nap. But napping has never ever been his thing, even when he's very sleepy.

But today was somehow different. Here they are...both fast asleep at the same time. How did I do it? I don't know. Can I do it again tomorrow. Absolutely not. This is a once in a lifetime thing. Or even if I am able to replicate this at some point, it won't be for a very long time.

So I should sleep. I really should. That's what my mom would tell me, and she's absolutely right. But here I am, eight months pregnant, and this little baby in my belly thinks he's a gymnast. He's tumbling and jumping and practicing his cartwheels. My uterus just isn't that big, but he cares not. Every few moments, he throws a punch at my belly button and kicks me in the ribs.

And Toren, the one who despises sleep, is passed out on my arm and it's so numb I'm not convinced I have anything past an elbow. I've tried wiggling my fingers, but they're very tingly and don't want to move much. Miela is sleeping on my leg and I can't feel that either. I could use any support, anything at all, for my low back. I'm kind of doing a weird sit-up and I'm failing at it. My neck is cranked in a weird way. But I can't move my head at all. If I do, I risk collapsing from this weird sit-up and then these two might roll off of me and onto the ground, and that would certainly bring about a wild fit of screaming and crying from them.

Man, I'd kill for a burrito, or even some goldfish at this point. It's too much to even imagine I could get water, or any type of liquid actually. Chapstick? Some socks? Not a chance.

Miela demands that she falls asleep with her finger in my belly button, so whenever I'm trying to put her down, I have to roll up my shirt, expose my massive, pregnant belly and let her very uncomfortably poke her little finger right in my belly button. It's the same belly button that this baby in my belly is punching on repeat. These two are working together, I just know it. And this exposed tummy is actually cold. There's a blanket right by my foot...I can touch it with my big toe...it's so close, but still it's too far away.

So I won't nap. I won't even move. I'm not messing this moment up. It's far too glorious to ruin. This is the epitome of nap-trapped.

. . . .

Just like babies are all different, mothers are all different too. So, not everything works for everyone.

We used to have the sweetest old lady as a neighbor when we lived in Hillcrest in San Diego. We were on the 6th floor of a high rise building and she was down the hall from us. Ellie, that was her name. Ellie and I were

     Treading Water, Holding Weights

good buds. When I had my first child, I would stop by a few days a week, usually when the afternoons were feeling very long and I needed another adult to talk to. She asked how we were sleeping at night and I told her that my husband and I were exhausted. Our son was six months old and we unintentionally started co-sleeping and it was a little rough, but we were working it out. She was floored that we'd bring our baby into our bed and adamantly expressed her concern about this to me. She didn't understand how a marriage could handle having a baby sleeping in bed too. She told me we'd never have sex again until that baby was out of the bed and back in his crib. But co-sleeping felt pretty right for us and we had worked out the logistics surrounding intimacy, so it wasn't a huge deal. But she brought it up every single time I stopped by, like it was a huge mistake and we were just too young to understand.

Families are all different, too. So not everything works for everyone.

I believe that we, as mothers, have to be mindful about whom we go to for advice. Find the sources you trust, the ones who are really looking out for you, and make them your go to people when you need advice. Find the experts who resonate with your approach to parenting. Seek out the moms who have been in your shoes and understand what you're trying to accomplish. Those are your people.

And when the guy at the gas pump leans over and tells you that you need to show your kids who's boss when they don't listen to you for the 7th time in a row, let it roll off your back. You can't control who offers you advice, what they say or how they say it, but you can control how you respond to it. That's the power you do have.

The advice that gets tossed around and the messages it sends to women can be really tough. It's easy to take advice, even the well-intended and useful stuff, and feel like it somehow means we aren't doing things right, or we aren't good enough mothers. The insecurities in motherhood can get heavy if we aren't careful.

So guard yourself carefully. Sift through the advice. Welcome in the useful, well-intended pieces and feel free to escort the rest of it right out of your mind. Don't harbor resentment towards those who sling unsolicited advice your way. That resentment isn't going to do you any good anyways.

And sometimes we have to decide to unlearn the things we think we are supposed to do in motherhood that aren't working out for us anymore. I bet you are doing some things the way you do them because that's how your mom did them when you were little, so it seems like the right thing to do. But maybe these things need to be unlearned and released. Often we need to make a conscious decision to go against the way things have always been done or the things we have always been told because, frankly, they aren't working for us.

Pay attention to your life. Notice the things that are serving you in motherhood and the things that are not. Does something need to change? If yes, then change it. Don't wait for someone to tell you to change it. Don't wait for the walls to come crashing down around you to make changes. Make them now.

I was just talking to a mom friend of mine about how both of our moms strongly believe that we need to instill a little fear into our children. We've each heard from our mothers, repeatedly, that it's really important for children to have a little fear of their parents. I've heard this for years. I've thought about this. I've considered using this approach. I've tried it a little bit. But it doesn't feel right for me. It worked for my mom. It doesn't work for me. So I'm unlearning that one.

. . . sometimes we have to decide to unlearn the things we think we are supposed to do in motherhood that aren't working out for us anymore.

TREADING WATER, HOLDING WEIGHTS

INSTAGRAM POST FEBRUARY 13, 2019

My mom goes by many names in our house: Nana (Karoh), Jamma Joan (Miela), Ms. Madden (Toren, because he is always moving too quickly to even keep names straight) and I'm Losing My Mind (that would be me...that's when my mom knows to step in and save the day).

She's been here a week and we have her for one more. We haven't gotten out of the house much. Sometimes I forget to feed her. I've thrown my kids her way a number of times, grabbed my bag and tip-toed out of the house. We make her sleep in the kids' room. She does dishes and changes diapers and cleans up the toys that magically appear all over my house all day long, everywhere, with no end, ever. Our house wakes up early. Like, 5am. My baby wakes up earlier. Like, 3:45am. So I'm rocking zombie mom status right now, which comes with a heavy dose of craziness.

I also recently decided to take on a couple of clients, which has turned into more than a couple. So I'm sorting out what this new schedule looks like for us while my mom is here, silently saving the day left and right.

One of my favorite things about her right now is that she sees the craziness I am balancing and, instead of trying to solve it all for me, she supports me in whatever way she can. Instead of judging me for making what she might consider questionable decisions, she's right by my side supporting those questionable decisions because they are the things I have chosen to do. Instead of telling me what I'm doing wrong, she's telling me I'm a great mom and that I have great kids.

Thank you Mom, I don't hear that or think that enough, and sometimes I forget it's the truth.

All of our visitors tell us we live at a wild pace. We exhaust anyone who comes to stay with us. Planning a trip to visit the Carlsbad Kushnaryovs isn't a vacation. It's a commitment.

Also, yes, that is a child under that plastic bin. Hey, whatever works Jamma Joan. You do what you need to do.

. . . .

Now, my mom is brilliant in so many areas of mothering, and I've never been as close to her as I am now. I live across the country from her, but I call her almost daily. She has been a tremendous source of strength, sanity and wisdom for me while I've learned the ins and outs of motherhood. But there are most definitely things she did with her six children that I have decided not to do with mine. I know that when I go to her for advice, she's coming at it from her own perspective on how motherhood goes. I have to keep that in mind.

It's like this for absolutely everyone we get advice from. Other peoples' advice isn't the law, but sometimes we take it that way.

You choose. Get the advice you want from the people you want, and then you decide what works for you, your baby and your family.

So let's take this opportunity to review this little list:

　　　　　TREADING WATER, HOLDING WEIGHTS

**26 Crappy Things People Say to Moms All the Time,
and What They Should Say Instead**

For some reason, people seem to rip off the filters on their mouths when speaking to mothers. It's like everyone out there thinks mothers are constantly looking for advice from anyone at any time and always. But we aren't actually looking for advice from anyone at any time and always. Here's what everyone out there SHOULD NOT be saying, WHY they should not be saying it and what they SHOULD be saying instead:

1. Treasure every moment. It all goes by so fast.
    - Do not say this because it is absolutely impossible to treasure all of the moments, particularly the ones that involve poop, vomit, tantrums and exhaustion.
    - Say this instead: "I've ordered your family dinner tonight. It'll be delivered around 5pm."
2. It's too cold for them to be outside. They'll catch a cold!
    - Do not say this because it's ludicrous and is code for "You aren't dressing your children appropriately." No mom wants to hear that.
    - Say this instead: "I can see that your children really love you."
3. Sleep when the baby sleeps.
    - Do not say this because anxiety and chores and to-do lists are all very real. We'll sleep when the baby sleeps when we can start folding laundry when the baby folds laundry.
    - Say this instead: "You are an amazing mother."
4. You shouldn't work full-time. Your kids need you.
    - Do not say this because, for whatever reason, many moms work. They choose it or they have to do it or their sanity depends on it. Whatever their reason is, it is none of your business. Being away from children is not easy, and they don't need to be reminded of that.
    - Say this instead: "You have really great kids."

5. The days are long but the years are short.

    • Do not say this because the days can be really really really long and
      the years can feel long too. Telling mothers that the years are short,
      while you may have good intentions, doesn't feel great to hear. It
      makes us think 'Oh man, I should be loving it all. What's wrong with
      me? Why am I NOT loving it all?' No one needs that pressure.
    • Say this instead: "Oh my goodness, you look radiant today!"

6. Oh! Put socks on that baby.

    • Do not say this because it's not your baby and so those feet are not
      yours either.
    • Say this instead: "I have two free hours on Saturday, and I thought I'd
      come by to wash your floors."

7. Well, you sure have your hands full.

    • Do not say this because the mother you're saying it to absolutely
      has her hands full, and she is reminded of it every single moment of
      every day, without you even saying it. It would be like if every time
      you walked out of the house, someone said to you "Oh, look! You
      have a foot."
    • Say this instead: "I have this extra gift certificate for a pedicure. Here
      you go."

8. Oh, you look tired.

    • Do not say this because we all look in mirrors every day, and moms
      do not need to be reminded that the chronic exhaustion they're suf-
      fering from is taking its toll on their looks. They already know it.
    • Say this instead: "I really like your shoes."

9. Let your baby cry a little. It's good for them.

    • Do not say this because a mother is the one who decides how much
      she will let her baby cry. Also, are you really sure it's "good for
      them"? I mean, would it be "good for you" if I saw you crying on the
      side of the street and I was like "Oh, just let them cry. It's good for
      them, I'm sure."
    • Say this instead: "I'll come over and fold all of your laundry on
      Thursday."

    TREADING WATER, HOLDING WEIGHTS

10. Can't you get your kid to behave?
    - Do not say this because children are chaos, and trying to get them to always behave is like trying to hold a gallon of water in a coffee filter while a band of hysterical gypsy rats nips at your heels.
    - Say this instead: "Your kids have adorable smiles."

11. It looks like you've lost all of that baby weight.
    - Do not say this because it's just a horrible thing to say. In fact, I'd steer clear of body comments entirely. I get it. You're trying to pay a compliment. But it comes with too many layers.
    - Say this instead: "Did you get stuck in all of that traffic on 2nd Street? What was going on? Was everyone trying to get to the movie theater at once?!"

12. You aren't breastfeeding? or You're still breastfeeding?
    - This is such a personal decision that comes with a lot of feelings. Some moms feel pride about their breastfeeding choices, and some feel tremendous amounts of guilt and inadequacy. Sometimes, whether you're still breastfeeding or not may not be a choice you even got to make. It can be a choice that is made for moms. So don't tread lightly here. Just don't tread at all.
    - Say this instead: "I'm going to come over and hold your baby while you take a shower. Just let me know when."

13. Should your child be doing that?
    - Ok, if it's a matter of life or death, you can chime in here. But for the most part, let the mother do the mothering. Believe it or not, we see everything. If we're letting our kids do something, chances are that, yes, our child should be doing that.
    - Say this instead: "You're a really great mother."

14. You kid is so small. Are they getting enough to eat?

    - Do not say this because we're analyzing our kids all the time, even when we're trying not to. Getting our kids to eat the stuff we want them to eat is kind of like trying to get a flock of chickens to swim across a pool in a straight line. But we try anyways, daily. So, no, they probably aren't getting enough to eat or they probably aren't eating perfectly. But, man, we sure are trying, so no need to check in on this one.
    - Say this instead: "You have a happy kid. You're doing something right."

15. Can't you just get a sitter?

    - Do not say this because it's not always that easy, but saying it like that implies that it should be, which makes us feel like we are doing something wrong, once again.
    - Say this instead: "Let's go somewhere that's kid-friendly at a time that works for you guys."

16. Don't you do anything for yourself? (meaning something without the kids, like self-care or a hobby or something)

    - Do not say this because balancing motherhood with the rest of our identity as a mother is a thing we're always navigating, and it can be more complicated than just doing "anything for yourself" implies. The thought of a little self-care or pursuing a hobby can feel like such a distant reality to mothers who are working tirelessly to keep the mom ship afloat. If you want to talk about the many facets of the woman, that's a conversation to have over tea, with screaming children running around. You'll need to schedule it with that mom four weeks in advance, send reminder text messages and expect her to cancel on you 13 times. But, at some point, the conversation can be had and the tea can be consumed and the children can run around screaming.
    - Say this instead: "Let's go on a walk if you feel up for it. I'll push the stroller."

17. One day you're going to miss this.

   - Do not say this because the guilt that comes with it is so heavy. It's like saying "You better enjoy all of the moments and everything about this entirely, even the excruciatingly impossible times, or you will grow old and regret it all and then you'll die with all of these regrets piled up on you and your final breaths will be inhaled and exhaled through the crushing regrets that are stacked upon your chest." Or something like that.
   - Say this instead: "Let me know if I can help you, even if it's just holding a baby while you tie your shoes."

18. I hate to tell you, but it gets worse.

   - Do not say this because the mother hearing it is thinking one of two things. She's either thinking that you're too old to remember all of the lows that come with the highs of raising little ones. Or she's thinking "Great, thanks. I should just die now." You don't want to say something that's going to point out how old you are or how impossible someone's life is, right?
   - Say this instead: "I'm going to come over and wash your baseboards."

19. He's a bit of a handful, huh?

   - Do not say this because no mom needs someone else pointing out that their child is a handful. It's like an insult to the child and a little slap in the face to the mother, and no one should go around insulting children and slapping moms.
   - Say this instead: "I made some homemade granola and I know your kids love this stuff. I'll leave it at your door this afternoon and won't even ring the doorbell. You keep the tupperware."

20. Oh, are they not talking/sitting/walking/reading yet?
    • Do not say this because moms are already pretty analytical of their children's developmental milestones. Sometimes those yearly check-ups to the doctor can be tough. The pediatrician asks "So, is he saying at least 20 words." And we're thinking 'Oh crap no! He just drools and eats his feet.' but we respond: "Oh, absolutely. I'm not sure why he won't talk now. He's just shy. But he totally talks a ton at home." So when you check in on their developmental milestones in such a condescending way, it just rattles us to the bones. There are enough things in motherhood rattling our bones, so please keep it to yourself. You can journal privately about it at night if you really need to ask those questions.
    • Say this instead: She's got the sweetest feet.
21. Your children need to fear you a little.
    • Do not say this because, well, do they actually need to fear us? I mean, do they really? Are mothers supposed to be an unending source of true love, the deepest affection and a place of complete safety sprinkled with just a little bit of absolutely terrifying fear. Is that what we are?
    • Say this instead: "Oh my gosh, did you see that bird?"
22. Just wait until they're teenagers. That's when the real work begins.
    • Don't say this because it's not true. No, no it's not. The real work has already begun, and moms are in the midst of the real work no matter how old their child is. This is all REAL WORK, for real.
    • Say this instead: I like the way your kid explores the world, and I can't wait to watch them grow up.
23. Your baby cries a lot.
    • Do not say this because babies are supposed to cry. Some cry more than others, and some cry less than others. It's like blinking. Some people blink more than others, and some people blink less than others. It's fine. Plus, moms hear their babies cry. We can hear it from a distance when no one else can. We're so dialed in. So we know how much our baby is crying, and no one needs to let us know if they think our baby cries too much or blinks too much. We got it.
    • Say this instead: "If you'd like me to hold your crying baby and walk around, I'd be more than happy to."

24. My kids never did that.
    - Do not say this because your kids DID do that. Or if it wasn't that exactly, it was something else. But your kid did some version of THAT. You just forgot.
    - Say this instead: "Here, I brought you some coffee."
25. You're already going back to work?
    - Do not say this because it implies that the mother doesn't care that much about her baby, and that she is choosing to be at a job instead of home snuggling her sweet little human being. It's also implying that she's doing something wrong and that you know better than her. It's also making her feel like a bad mom and deepening the layers of mom guilt that have already begun to build up. I don't think this is what you're trying to do, so just save this one for your journal too.
    - Say this instead: "You have a lot of strength, and I admire that in you."
26. You're so lucky you get to stay at home with them.
    - Do not say this because many stay at home moms feel like their souls are being sucked out of them and their lives are foggy, black and white cartoons playing on a tv from the 1960s that was recently hit by a hammer. But, it also has its glorious, beautiful moments, just like working moms experience. Isn't it strange how both working moms and stay at home moms can experience such a vast array of emotions about how they're spending their days? I don't think luck plays a part though.
    - Say this instead: "Want a beer?"

Advice can be golden. It can also be really painful to hear.

CHAPTER THIRTEEN

Care About Your Body: Just do it for the right reasons and in the right way.

Let's talk about boobs. If you're a guy you may be like 'Oh come on, boobs?' Or actually, maybe you're like 'Oh come on!! Boobs!!' Who knows. But for the moms out there, you'll get this.

I'm 26 weeks pregnant and a couple of weeks ago, my boobs got the memo that we're producing another human being and immediately jumped to attention. They screamed 'Oh yeah! We've done this before! We're ready! Let's go!'

And I was like 'Hold on girls. I don't need you yet. It's too early.'

And they were like 'Yeah, whatever. Here we are! We are ready to go!'

To which I responded, 'Oh, you're ready now? Suddenly you're big and perky and I have cleavage? Where the hell were you last summer when I was trying on swimsuits, huh? Sit down.'

And they had nothing to say to me, because there was nothing to say.

Then my arms started to get excited, and they got bigger too. And I was like 'Hey! Hold on! What the hell do you think you're doing? This isn't about you!'

And they were like 'But those two are getting bigger. We want to, too. We can do that. Give us a chance.'

'The heck you can! This is not about you. Stay right where you are,' I hollered back.

And they weren't happy with me, so they got bigger just to spite me, and because they have been waiting for their chance.

Every time I'm pregnant, I'm both in awe of how astoundingly amazing my body is and absolutely completely horrified, all at the same time. Tell me, body, how is it that you can grow bigger than I ever thought possible, then smile at me slyly, whisper in my ear 'hold my beer' and grow even bigger. You sprint through those adorable baby bump days and head right for the giant whale phase. And there you just hang out, casually as if it's all ok. But it's not ok right now because I can't shave my bikini line and I'd like to for absolutely no reason.

Once when I was nine months pregnant, I realized that my belly made a perfectly good kitchen table. So I sat down, put my plate on my belly and enjoyed my meal. It comes in handy, this growing belly. But I am looking forward to the day when I can get in and out of my car at the store without being pancaked between my car and the car next to me. No matter how much room I think I've left myself to wiggle through, it is never enough. I find myself wedged between car doors, shimmying my large self toward freedom. I am a grown woman and I need to maintain some shred of dignity here. Instead, I find myself doing a side shuffle while my belly wipes down the side of the neighboring car. I'm like a free partial car wash. You're welcome, people of Carlsbad. You're welcome.

Body image is a tough one to swallow when you become a mom. The more kids you have, the harder it becomes. On the inside, I still feel so much like the 23 year old version of myself, running down the beaches of Australia with a killer bod, comfortably wearing that little bikini. On the outside, things have changed.

But this body has grown human beings inside of it, four of them actually, and that is not a small feat. It's epic. And as the years tick by, I have been finding it harder and harder to keep everything toned and the cellulite at bay.

I was watching the Taylor Swift documentary on Netflix tonight. I've never been a hardcore Swift fan, but decided to watch some of it while the kids were falling asleep in their beds. The woman is pretty amazing and her honesty and candid descriptions of everything she's gone through were refreshing. Here's a woman who seems to have it all (but I know that no one does, or maybe we all do, most of us just have a convoluted definition of what "having it all" means) and she still struggles with body image.

          TREADING WATER, HOLDING WEIGHTS

. . . we are all so conditioned to attack ourselves and tear our bodies down.

She still stares at photos of herself and sees a long list of flaws that have spiraled her into eating disorder struggles.

It reminded me that we are all so conditioned to attack ourselves and tear our bodies down. Instead of honoring these fabulous vessels for all that they do, we find flaws and feel shame.

There is another mother whom I run into about once every two months. We both have young kids and our paths usually cross somewhere in the neighborhood or at a function. Every time I see her, one of the first things she tells me is that I look like I have lost weight. Every. Single. Time. I met her right after having my 3rd baby, like a couple of weeks after. I've shed those pregnancy pounds since then, but I always feel this horrible heaviness when she comments on my weight. I can't help but think, 'Wait, are you saying I was fat before?' And then I start asking myself if I was really fat or if it took me too long to lose those baby pounds or if I should exercise more or maybe eat only kale for lunch.

I have to pull myself out of this. You do too if this is where you find yourself going.

These bodies are glorious and deserve to be treated well. The number on the scale or the way our butts look in our skinny jeans shouldn't matter.

We need to shift the way we look at ourselves. It's time to take a step back. Instead of judging your body on its looks, get in touch with how your body is feeling and operating to get a better grasp on what's going on. Stop asking yourself these questions:

Is my waist small enough? Are my boobs big enough? Am I tall enough? Do I have cellulite? Do I look fat? Are my arms the right size?

What if we instead asked ourselves these questions:

Am I able to wake up in the morning energized? Can I still run and play with my kids? Do I feel healthy and vibrant in this body? Can I walk and swim and bike (or whatever it is you want to be doing) without pain? Does my body feel nourished and fueled? Is this body able to live the life I want to be living?

Exercise and nutrition are important. We shouldn't ignore them. But the purpose of going to the gym and eating the right foods is not to look skinny. No. The purpose is to feel alive and energetic so that we can live this life the way we want to live it.

He grabbed me and pulled me down and said, 'Dear god you're heavy. What have you been eating on the farm all month?!'

The only answer I could think of: garlic. But then again, it's Wisconsin and there's bread and cheese and a lack of nearby Orangetheories. But that garlic harvest was a sweat fest and jogging down those country roads zaps you.

I find that there are different scales in life these days: Can I still climb trees and run with chickens and pick through berry bushes in the mosquito-filled evening? Can I make a valiant effort at a game of sharks and minnows in the evening and run a solid 5K in the morning? Can I beat my kids at a water balloon toss and do a legit somersault on the lawn? Can I carry all of my kids when the asphalt is too hot? Can I harvest 14,000 heads of garlic and still run with my kids through the slip 'n slide to cool off?

If so, I'm good.

Getting back to my routines will feel so good when we finally find our way back to California. But for now, routines are long gone, bedtimes are always missed, naps are a bonus and no one is wearing shoes or pants.

. . . .

I wonder what we'd say to our children if they said about themselves the same things we say about ourselves. Think of the last time you looked at yourself in the mirror and weren't thrilled with what you saw. What message did you send yourself? What was your self-talk? Now imagine your child saying that out loud about themselves. What would you tell them? That's what you need to be telling yourself.

Be gentle and compassionate with yourself. Your body is an amazing thing that can do wonders if it's treated well. But you can't rely on the world around you to define the relationship you're going to have with your body. You must do that.

The purpose is to feel alive and energetic so that we can live this life the way we want to live it.

Don't cash in your chips on your health and fitness. It's important stuff. But understand WHY it's important. We want a lot of years on this earth so that we can watch these beautiful babies grow up and live their lives, right? We want to be around for all of the amazing things that the future holds. That is why we need to focus on our health. It's not so that we can still fit into those shorts that we wore when we were 20 years old and have been hanging on to.

CHAPTER FOURTEEN

Pick Your Battles: If you make everything a battle, everything is hard.

In life, we get to pick and choose what we'll stand up for and what we'll let slide. The same goes for motherhood, and that's a pretty cool thing. Boundaries and rules are great for kids, obviously. They need to know what's ok and what's not, so that they can grow up to be good humans.

When my oldest was two, I was having a hard time setting boundaries for him and then sticking to them. It was easy to tell him "don't do that thing or else you'll lose this privilege", but I wasn't always great at following through. My mom chimed in one day and told me to just pick three things that I was going to make firm rules in the house for him, and then never ever crumble on those rules.

Picking three things was manageable for me because I could remember them and I could actually enforce them. Three things was also manageable for him because he was only two years old and that was about all his brain could keep straight. It was so much better than my previous approach, which was hurling rules out left and right whenever it felt like it made sense to me. That way of doing things just confused me, and it confused him too. And then, everything started to feel hard.

So we simplified and the rules felt clear and the friction felt a little lighter.

JOURNAL ENTRY JUNE 13, 2019

Sad Mother Monkey

Lately my kids are doing this amazing thing. They're all playing together. Actually, they're playing next to each other and sometimes with each other. Sometimes it's not playing at all, it's just fighting. But the point is that they're doing it together, right? I don't know. But whatever. I just love that they all squish together like a pile of tadpoles. Karoh turns one this week. It feels like he was born yesterday. It also feels like he's been here for 10 years. How is that possible?

Yesterday I caught Miela rubbing salami all over her hair. How is THAT possible? Actually WHY is that possible? What makes someone decide that's a good idea? There had to be an internal dialogue that went something like this 'Oh, salami! I should rub this all over my head.' What kind of a person decides that's a good idea?

Yesterday Toren convinced Miela that her favorite song was Sad Mother Monkey and she believed him. She screamed at me for 10 minutes in the car to play Sad Mother Monkey. I would gladly have said yes. I totally would make that happen for her. My kids are definitely the dj's in the car. But it's not a real song. Sad Mother Monkey doesn't exist. Check Spotify. It's not there. But Toren said it was her favorite song, so it was her favorite song. It was my word against his, and apparently my word didn't hold up very well in this battle. I mean, come on. Imagine that song. Say it out loud. It's absurd.

My baby is walking. My five year old is writing sentences. My two year old smells like salami. I say we're winning today.

Yesterday we weren't winning. We had to get my mom on FaceTime to teach Miela about serious head injuries in an effort to get her to stop hitting Karoh over the head with anything she can get her hands on. I cannot turn my back on the two of them for a second. But hurting other people is a pretty firm "NO" in my book, so we have to keep at this one and hope that one day it will start to sink in, and she'll ease up on the baby.

Miela is perhaps her best self at the beach. The other day she stood on a sand pile and yelled, 'Toren, you have to begin to begin every day.' Then she ran to me, jumped in my lap and said, 'Mama, you look like a rainbow.'

I can't keep up, but I'm not even trying to anymore. Let's just keep everyone alive.

. . . .

We can't always choose the path of least resistance in parenting. We have to do the hard thing sometimes, like taking away privileges that are hard to take away or following through with discipline when it's really inconvenient for us to do that. But there's a lot of value in doing the hard thing when it needs to be done.

The trick, in my opinion, is in choosing the battles that need to be fought, and taking a stand on the matters with our children that we really feel strongly about. Otherwise, our entire day can easily turn into a struggle.

. . . there's a lot of value in doing the hard thing when it needs to be done.

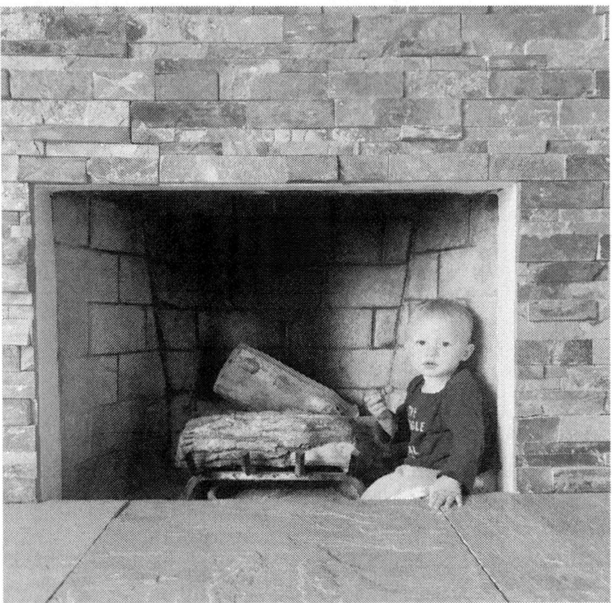

The baby is in the fireplace again

Last week I walked into the living room to find Karoh, my 1 year old, sitting in the fireplace. I gave him a look that said 'Kid, get out of the fireplace.' He looked back at me with a face that said 'No, mom, I got this.' I gave him a final look that said 'Ok, fine, whatever.' Then I turned around to do the dishes. This is the kind of thing that happens with the third child.

The third child is amazingly resilient. I've seen him fall off furniture, do an army roll and jump back to his feet in 3 seconds. The third child is quite good at catching on to things like common sense and caution, too. I spent weeks pulling him out of the fireplace. It was exhausting, so I finally gave up. We never use the fireplace, so it's probably pretty clean, but it just looks bad having your kid sit in the fireplace. I'm like 'Yo, dude, we have couches and carpet and even some little chairs. Do you have to sit in the fireplace.' But he does. That's exactly where he wants to be.

One day I gave up on this battle and let him win. Here you go kid, this one goes to you. How about I win that battle we're having about keeping you out of the street? That's not one I'm willing to give up on. But you can have the fireplace. It's all yours. Want me to serve you meals in there? Would you like to take your naps in there? I can work with this.

The other day I walked into the kids' room to find Miela, his big sister, hitting him on top of the head repeatedly. I was about to intervene when he gave me a little smile and then bit her foot. Sometimes I think he's just a little baby and sometimes I realize he's basically almost 12.

. . . .

I think this idea of picking your battles can be used in a broader context, beyond how we handle our children. And perhaps we can soften the word "battles" into something like "focus" for this instance.

A good friend of mine was at a couples retreat with her husband. She is a stay at home mom, and there were a few other stay at home moms and dads at the retreat as well. The topic came up about the amount of pressure they feel to keep a clean house, make a delicious meal and also find the time to shower and look decent every single day before their spouses come home from work. I can relate to this on some level. Maybe you can too.

The retreat leader had some legit advice. She told them that each day, they should just choose one of those things, and maybe even let their spouse know which was the focus for that day. If they were going to make a good meal, the house could be a mess and so could they. But maybe they were hoping to be intimate that night, then dinner was a frozen pizza and the house was in shambles. However, a shower happened and that breath was fresh.

I sometimes find myself going back to this little tip and using it when I feel like I'm failing on all fronts. It's a great reminder that I can't necessarily do it all well, but I can do some of it well, and I should pick what I want to focus on in order to make sure I'm putting my energy where I want to shine. Otherwise, everything starts to turn into a battle, and then everything is hard.

CHAPTER FIFTEEN

Go Easy on Yourself: You deserve a break, but it has to start with you.

In my many conversations with mothers from all different walks of life, I find that we have a few things in common:

1. We are all working so incredibly hard to be the best mothers we can possibly be.
2. We all struggle with mom guilt at times.
3. We are all far too hard on ourselves.
4. We all love our children deeply.

This isn't an easy gig, but it's an awesome one. Since becoming a mom, I've found a strength within myself that I never knew I had. My ability to drag myself out of bed when I'm absolutely, shockingly exhausted and still take care of my children in the middle of the night is the type of thing legends are made of.

I can multi-task like a freaking pro. Singing "Row Row Row Your Boat" to my toddler while at the same time nursing a baby, making a lasagna, correcting math homework, wiping a snotty nose and answering a barrage of questions about the Bermuda Triangle is just a standard glimpse into my superhuman day.

And I bet all moms have their own version of this.

We are amazing. We are prepared for most major disasters at all times. We can anticipate our children's needs well before they have a clue that they even need something. If you were going to be stranded on a desert island and could only bring one thing, you should definitely choose to bring a mother with you. Almost any mother would do. She could keep you fed, clothed, adequately rested and completely entertained with whatever foliage the island had to offer until a rescue boat found you.

. . . .

JOURNAL ENTRY OCTOBER 22, 2019

Magical household items

It was a long grocery shopping trip with an exhausted baby, a super dramatic and needy toddler who wouldn't keep her shirt on, and a six year old boy on wheelie shoes with the energy of a firecracker in a mason jar. After much work and patience, I found myself at the check out counter, searching for my wallet that was buried deep in my purse. I dug and dug, but there was nothing. Could you imagine getting this far and not being able to walk out those doors with your groceries because you left your wallet on the kitchen counter when you took it out to find your kid's insurance card?

Could you even imagine? It must be one of my worst nightmares because the grocery store is a place that requires grit, strength and resolve. Getting that close to the finish line only to find out that it was all for nothing is the kind of thing that causes panic attacks and hospitalization.

I threw my hand in one more time, determined to emerge with that wallet. I started pulling out the contents of my purse and putting them on the counter: a pile of plastic peas, a long beaded necklace with a shark's tooth, a plastic dinosaur, a lollipop (you never know when those will come in handy, but when you need them, you're so glad you have them) and a very dirty baby wipe that looked scary. I plunged my hand back in. One sock for the trampoline park, a bag of play-doh, half of an orange and a very hairy giant fake spider. I placed it all on the counter and went back in. There was that other sock and finally, there was my wallet.

These moments seem totally normal at first, but then you look around you and quickly realize that your reality is not at all normal. In fact, most adults would struggle to walk in your shoes for 10 minutes because the baggage that comes with walking in your shoes for 10 minutes is bizarre, disgusting and very confusing.

But that moment when your toddler is losing his mind and you reach into your purse and pull out a pile of plastic peas, that moment is glorious and considered a huge MOM WIN because sometimes only a pile of plastic peas will soothe him. Or a bag of play-doh or a horrible fake spider.

Motherhood requires a lot creativity when it comes to normal household items. We were on a walk the other day with my massive double Bob stroller and I looked down through the little window in the sunshade that gives you a quick peek at your kids. I like to keep this window closed because if I use my imagination, I can kind of imagine I'm alone on these walks, except for the massive double Bob that I'm pushing. If they can't see me, I'm kind of alone. I love taking walks with my kids, don't get me wrong here. But I also love pushing a stroller of quiet children while enjoying a few minutes of sunshine and silence.

But when I did gaze through the window, I saw a variety of items stuffed in the sides of the stroller. We had grilling tongs, a turkey baster, one of my running shoes, a tube of toothpaste and a tampon. All of these things were collected by my children and very carefully placed in the sides of the stroller without me realizing it.

I'm not sure how they do it. But I imagine them walking through the house thinking 'Mom said we're going on a walk, what do we need?' One of them sees the grilling tongs and immediately yells to the other 'Quick, those! We NEED those! Get them. Don't let her see you.' And I bet the other says 'Ok and you go in that bottom drawer in mom's bathroom and get one of those wrapped up, long, skinny colorful things. We NEED that!' I don't know how they do this, but they do.

And somehow I'm too busy collecting snacks, making sure bladders are empty and filling water bottles to notice what's going on.

. . . .

But the thing that continues to amaze me is how hard we are on ourselves. Moms are so critical of their decisions. We tend to second guess ourselves far too much. There is this amazing thing that we have called a mother's intuition. When we can really tap into this, we tend to make the best decisions for ourselves and for our children. But in a world where we're being sent so many messages about what we should or shouldn't do and how we should or shouldn't raise our children, tapping into this intuition is so hard. It becomes nearly impossible to really tune into this voice within us and to embrace, without question, the decisions we know deep down to be best for ourselves and our families.

I firmly believe that the entire family functions much better when the mother is in a good place. We sit at the center of it all, and everyone else's energy feeds off of our energy. Sounds kind of exhausting, right? Not only do we have to keep people fed, diapers clean and make sure our kids are doing their homework, but we also have to make sure our own energy is in a good place so that everyone else can be in a good place too.

Now, this doesn't mean that we have to be happy and smile 100% of the time, definitely not. And this doesn't mean that we can't have hard days or weeks or even months. It also doesn't mean that if we are in a good mood, everyone else will automatically follow suit and the whole household will be chipper. It definitely doesn't mean any of that.

But it does mean that we are a rock in the family, a solid foundation and a source of stability and endless love. We carry a lot on our shoulders, and we rise to so many challenges. We are amazing, and our children rely on us for much more than school lunches and rides to soccer practice.

Unfortunately, so many moms are so critical of themselves. Many of us tend to slip into an unhealthy, harsh internal dialogue on a daily basis. Instead of commending ourselves and lifting ourselves up, we are quick to feel like we've failed in one way or another.

I challenge you to give yourself a break. Actually, give yourself many breaks. The next time you start to criticize yourself or feel guilty about something, stop yourself. Remind yourself that you, like every other mother out there, are doing your best. Tell yourself that you're a wonderful mother and that you love your children beyond words. Ease up on the expectations you have of yourself, the ones that always feel so impossible to meet. Choose a way that brings more ease and simplicity into your life.

This has to start with YOU. No one else is going to do this for you. It's time that you really dial into that self-talk you have going on in your head and weed out the negative stuff. Simplify your life, and don't be afraid to choose the path that feels like less friction from time to time. We all deserve a break.

. . . the entire family functions much better when the mother is in a good place.

CHAPTER SIXTEEN

The Lessons in Motherhood: The ones you want to learn, and the ones you'd kind of rather not.

I'm not afraid to admit that I'm not an expert in motherhood. Sure, I've written a book about it, but I find myself feeling like a beginner on a daily basis. Motherhood is the kind of thing that evolves the moment you think you've got it figured out. It's the kind of thing that teaches you new things over and over again, every day, if you're paying attention.

And be sure to pay attention. There are some pretty amazing life lessons buried in this pile of late night feedings, early morning wake-ups and temper tantrums in the grocery store. Motherhood brings about a wholeness in you and a perspective on life that is unlike any other.

So let's take a few minutes here to go over some of motherhood's best lessons, both the ones we are happy to learn and the ones we'd kind of rather not:

1. **The actual meaning of SELFLESSNESS:** When I was growing up, I never would have called myself selfish necessarily, (although my sister Megan would disagree). But I certainly wouldn't have called myself selfless. I think good ol' Megan may have actually nicknamed me "Melfish", an endearing combination of my name and the word "selfish". I don't know. Maybe I was just bold and fearless enough to go after the things I wanted. That sounds better than "selfish", right? Yeah. Let's go with that. But Motherhood has shown me what true selflessness is. It's given me a chance to be completely selfless in a way I never thought possible. The things

we moms will do for our children are astounding, and we never ask for anything in return. We give to them over and over again in so many ways. From the moment we first know of their existence, the sacrifices we make and the countless ways we put them first are endless.

2. **We are WAY STRONGER than we ever imagined:** There's that moment when you are so weary and haggard, when you can't even think straight and the world is a foggy mess. You are dead asleep. It's the middle of the night and you were just up one hour ago nursing your baby. You are so deeply asleep that you can't even dream. And then your newborn cries. You are needed. The eyelids open and somehow you muster up the strength to emerge from your cocoon of a bed. You stagger over to the crib and begin the late night, 45 minute feeding cycle once again. Somehow you do it even though it's an exhaustion so deep, one that you never knew could exist. Have you been there? This was most definitely me, many times. Or perhaps your super human strength showed up differently. Maybe you carried a toddler in one arm, a newborn in the other, groceries over your shoulders and made your way from the car to the house. Or perhaps it was leaving your baby and returning to work, which just may have been the hardest thing you've ever done. The list is really endless. Mothers show strength in a million ways every day, but it's not your typical strength. It's an emotional, physical and mental strength far greater than you ever could have imagined possessing before becoming a mom. But it's your strength, and you're amazing.

3. **Poop is actually not THAT horrible. I mean, it's horrible, but it's NOT the end of the world:** The other night I heard my daughter coughing non-stop in her bed in the middle of the night. She had a cold and it was one of those annoying ones where the post-nasal drip makes it impossible to sleep because you cough endlessly. I heard the coughing from my room, waited for it to stop, realized it wasn't going to and then went in to check on her. The moment I got to the door, she started making sounds like she was going to throw up. I ran to her with my arms outstretched and my hands together forming a little cup. I lunged at her just as she started to

vomit, and I miraculously caught most of it...in...my...hands. I saved the bedsheets—such a SUCCESS! But before motherhood, cupping handfuls of vomit in my hands would have been devastating to me. The amount of bodily fluids and other gross stuff moms deal with on the regular is alarming for the average person, but quite normal for us. Now, I'm not running around trying to wipe everyone's butt or catch throw up from the guy walking down the street, but there's something quite crazy about how totally ok it is to handle this stuff when it belongs to your kid. It's really not that bad.

4. **We have to say "no" to things, and we do not need an excuse to do so:** When you become a mom, your time becomes valuable in a new way. It's time to shamelessly prioritize things in your life and say NO to anything that doesn't make the cut. This is a lesson we usually learn the hard way. I remember my first year or two (or maybe four) of motherhood, I was notorious for saying yes to everything. I dragged my son to it all and he was actually pretty flexible. But it wore me out and totally overwhelmed me. Then I started turning things down. I started saying "NO" a lot and instead prioritizing things like sleep and relaxation and family time. If you haven't given the word "NO" a try, do it. It's miraculous and you don't have to come up with a super solid excuse to use it. Just use it.

5. **Taking care of ourselves is a priority, not a luxury:** This one is also hard to learn, but it's important. When the mom is worn out, everyone suffers. The day I found a restorative yoga and sound healing class that spoke to my soul was a really great day, for me AND my family. The day I started asking for help and stating my needs clearly to my husband was also a great day. It was kind of hard at first because everyone was used to me just being ok and taking care of it all. But it wasn't working for me. Something had to change. Mothers have an amazing ability to stretch themselves in a million ways at once, but it doesn't mean we should.

6. **P-A-T-I-E-N-C-E:** Oh, this was a hard lesson for me to learn. Actually, I'm seven years in on this whole mom thing and I'm STILL learning it. I've never in my life been a slow walker, but my children have short legs and their pace is excruciatingly slow at

times. I have to take a deep breath and take it down a few notches. Have you ever taught a child to use a scissors? I mean a kids' scissors, of course. It can be a very slow and challenging lesson. When I taught my son to do it, I just wanted to grab the paper and scissors and do it for him. But that wouldn't have been the lesson he needed. So instead, it became a valuable lesson for me in patience while he learned to cut snowflakes out of construction paper...a very slow and kind of painful lesson for me.

7. **The world is easier when we communicate in a healthy way:** This lesson definitely applies to everyone we communicate with, but particularly our spouses. My husband and I were shocked at the toll parenting took on our relationship. We both had our own style of doing things. We both had our own expectations and our own insecurities. There are a lot of different ways things like expectations and insecurities can come out in a conversation, and some of those ways are not exactly productive or healthy. We found ourselves arguing, caught up in our own stories on how things were going. This was a lesson we stumbled through in the early years and still find ourselves tripping over at times. But it has gotten better, thank goodness. Being able to really listen to each other and talk about what's going on is a game changer. This was a very good lesson to finally learn.

8. **Sleep is a priceless gift that we shouldn't squander:** The difference between Melissa on six hours of sleep and Melissa on eight hours of sleep is really shocking. I like myself a lot more on eight hours of sleep, and nine hours is even better. My kids wake up early, but for years I was still sticking to my pre-motherhood bed time. My head didn't hit the pillow until about 11pm, and my kids have never been good sleepers, so I was up at night. Then everyone was up by 6am for sure. It made me a shadow of myself for a very long time. Finally learning to embrace sleep and change my routine was amazing.

9. **Comparison takes all of the fun out of everything:** It's so easy to compare ourselves as mothers and our babies to others out there. But it's toxic. The quicker we learn this one, the better. Sure, we still might find ourselves walking into the comparison trap, but

     TREADING WATER, HOLDING WEIGHTS

once we've learned this lesson, we can quickly recognize what we're doing and stop.

10. **We really are enough already:** It's easy in motherhood to question everything you do, everything you say and everything you are. But once we learn that we are already enough, that we are deeply loved and doing our best, that's when we can release the unhealthy things like doubt and fear and guilt. Our identity goes through massive shifts when we take on the role of being a mother to someone. It can be confusing and also beautiful. Perhaps one of the greatest lessons is that we don't need to have the next step figured out in order to be a really amazing mother. I look at the way my children look at me and I am amazed with the amount of love we share. I'm already enough, and so are you.

Well, here's the thing really.

*This book is filled* with pages and pictures and stories. I'm one mom with one experience of motherhood. My hope is that you've read these pages and found a little more grace for yourself in motherhood. I hope you've loosened the reins of guilt and let go of some of your fears. In sharing my struggles and perhaps a few of my victories, as well as my tips and advice, I hope you've been able to see some of your own experience reflected in my version of motherhood.

Connecting with other moms is one of the greatest things we can do for ourselves to help us navigate these muddy waters. Because motherhood certainly gets muddy. It gets filthy, and having other women in your circle who get what you're going through is pretty amazing. I'd like to continue to be in your circle.

And here's the thing—your journey is your own, and everyone's is supposed to be unique to them. So embrace that. Own it. Make it your own and be proud of it, in all of its glory and chaos.

In the wise words of Mark Ricter, my father and a man whose parenting style includes a long string of one liners that he somehow applies to every situation, remember that "this too shall pass" and "you'll have a better day tomorrow" and maybe even "life is hard and then you die".

And in the wise words of my three year old daughter, Miela, "You have to begin to begin everyday."

xo Melissa

ABOUT THE AUTHOR

Hey, my name is Melissa. I'm the mother to four fabulous human beings who drive me nuts and make me laugh daily. My husband is a very unique, creative and sweet man. We both grew up in lovely Wisconsin, but now live in Carlsbad, CA with our two cats. I'm the Co-founder of a company called Seed & Song (www.seedandsong.com), that creates music, yoga and mindfulness experiences for moms, babies and toddlers.

I've never written a book before. This is my first one. But I write endlessly about motherhood. If you want to learn more about me, what I'm up to and what I'm writing, then hop on over to www.melissakushnaryov.com or find me on Instagram (melissakushnaryov).

I'm a Libra. I love farming. I keep my fingernails trimmed short. Pickled scapes are my favorite food right now. I don't know what else you could possibly need to know about me.

Made in the USA
Columbia, SC
21 September 2020